POLYOLEFIN PLASTICS

VAN NOSTRAND REINHOLD PLASTICS APPLICATIONS SERIES

POLYOLEFIN PLASTICS

THEODORE O. J. KRESSER

Chemicals Department
Gulf Oil Corporation
Orange, Texas

VAN NOSTRAND REINHOLD COMPANY
New York   Cincinnati   Toronto   London   Melbourne

Van Nostrand Reinhold Company Regional Offices:
Cincinnati, New York, Chicago, Millbrae, Dallas

Van Nostrand Reinhold Company Foreign Offices:
London, Toronto, Melbourne

Published by Van Nostrand Reinhold Company
450 West 33rd Street, New York, N.Y. 10001
Published simultaneously in Canada by
D. Van Nostrand Company (Canada), Ltd.

15 14 13 12 11 10 9 8 7 6 5 4 3 2 1

Van Nostrand Reinhold Plastics Applications Series

Allylic Resins and Monomers, *Harry Raech, Jr.*

Amino Resins, *John F. Blais*

Cellulosics, *Walter Paist*

Epoxy Resins, *Irving Skeist*

Gum Plastics, *M. Stafford Thompson*

Heat Sealing, *Robert D. Farkas*

High-Temperature Plastics, *Walter Brenner, Dorey Lum and Malcolm W. Riley*

Laminated Plastics (Second Edition), *D. J. Duffin*

Plastics Extrusion Technology (Second Edition), *Allan L. Griff*

Plastics Film Technology, *W. R. R. Park*

Polyamide Resins (Second Edition), *Don E. Floyd*

Polycarbonates, *William F. Christopher and Daniel W. Fox*

Polyester Resins, *John R. Lawrence*

Polyolefin Plastics, *T. O. J. Kresser*

Polystyrene, *William C. Teach and George C. Kiessling*

Polyurethanes (Second Edition), *Bernard A. Dombrow*

Polyvinyl Chloride, *Harold A. Sarvetnick*

Preface

This book is essentially a revision of the author's two previous books *Polyethylene* and *Polypropylene*. In the years that have passed since the publication of these books there has been a tremendous growth, not only in sales volume, but also in the complexity of the polyolefin plastics. Additional polyolefins have been introduced, and each original material has been developed into a whole series of materials, all with inherent similarities, but also with great practical differences. The result is a broad spectrum of plastics ranging from soft rubbery materials to hard, stiff and heat-resistant compounds.

In addition, polyolefin polymers very similar to the polymers which are the polyolefin plastics have found wide use outside the plastics field, as rubbers or elastomers on the one hand, and as fiber-forming materials on the other. These fields will not be covered in any detail, but we will consider them because there are many cases where the difference between plastics, and elastomers, or fibers is not clear.

The first task is therefore to define, as clearly as possible, what the subject of this book is, and what materials it will cover.

To make this clear, a genealogical chart of the polyolefin plastics has been prepared. It presents the materials in roughly chronological order of commercialization, from top to bottom. At the same time it shows the current materials across the bottom, the soft rubbery materials on the left, and the hard horny materials on the right. Horizontal connecting lines are used to show where a new polymer was a direct development from an earlier one.

Polyethylene is not only the oldest polyolefin polymer, but it is by far the largest in sales volume, and in its many modifications it now spans the entire property spectrum from soft and rubbery to hard and horny. In the polar copolymers it is spreading over into some traditional rubber applications, while on the hard side of the spectrum, it is used for some coarse fibers or *monofilaments,* also covering almost every traditional *plastics* application between.

The expansion of polypropylene applications has not been as extensive within the plastics spectrum itself. By means of copolymerization it has achieved greater toughness, especially at low temperature, when compared to its properties upon introduction, but the truly spectacular development has been outside the plastics field in fibers. After a slow start because of dyeing and finishing problems, polypropylene fiber, often called merely *olefin* fiber, is now the fastest growing synthetic fiber. It has a strong base in the carpet field that is rapidly being broadened to include general textile applications.

Copolymers of ethylene with other olefins have wide applications, and copolymers with polar monomers produce materials with unique and valuable properties. The most interesting of these, from a scientific point of view, are those made with ionizable monomers which can form compounds with metals and are generally called *ionomers*.

Polymers of higher olefins are now available. The two most prominent are polybutene-1, a tough semirigid material, and poly-4-methylpentene, which has the greatest heat resistance of all the polyolefins and is also glass clear. Many other polyolefins have been made and described but have not yet reached commercial development.

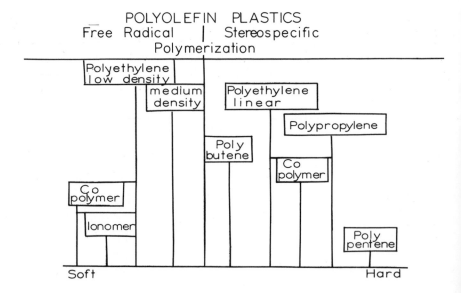

The other broad method of classifying polyolefins, as indicated in the accompanying chart, is the polymerization method. The first polyethylene was polymerized by a *free radical* method. This method is carried out at extremely high pressures and is initiated by peroxides, or other highly active substances which break up under reaction conditions to produce a highly energetic fragment called a free radical. This induces a very rapid, random linking of the ethylene into a high polymer. This method is used for the largest tonnages of polyethylene and also for a wide variety of copolymers.

The other method is the use of coordinating catalysts, usually solids, that join olefin molecules into a high polymer in a regular and highly controlled manner under moderate pressure. This method is usually carried out in the presence of a nonreactive hydrocarbon liquid which may, under the reaction conditions, dissolve the polymer formed (solvent process) or may not dissolve it (slurry or particle form process). The presence of the liquid is not essential to the process and it may be performed in pure gaseous olefin. The liquid is used as a carrier and temperature control medium.

The materials outlined above, their processing into useful products, and the applications of these products are covered in this book.

T. O. J. KRESSER

Orange, Texas
May 1969

Contents

ONE

historical development

MATERIALS

The modern polyolefin plastics are new materials, the first one being discovered only thirty-five years ago, but they are historically descended from a long line of plastic products.

Natural Materials

The first plastic products were naturally occurring materials, plant and insect resins both fresh and fossil, tars, asphalt and the drying oils, horn, tortoise shell, vegetable gums, and many others. The use of these materials established certain applications and developed processing techniques which led to the emergence of synthetic plastics. These were complex products whose origin and composition were little understood. They were used without modification or with some minor modification made on an empirical basis.

Modified Natural Materials

The next step towards a true synthetic plastic was the major chemical modification of a natural material. It is quite irrelevant whether we choose the addition of major amounts of sulfur to rubber to produce ebonite, still the best pipe stem material in the world, or whether we prefer the more generally accepted mixture of camphor and nitrocellulose to make celluloid. John Wesley Hyatt, the inventor of celluloid, is widely recognized as the father of the plastics industry. His claim is not based on a single invention, for he started the development to a remarkable extent of almost all of the modern plastics processing methods; he did not just invent a material but very nearly invented a whole industry.

In both of the above cases a complex and little understood natural product was modified by an entirely accidental discovery, which gave rise to an entirely different material of much greater usefulness.

The commercial value of the new products attracted the interests of scientists who sought to understand the basis of the useful properties. Chemistry up to that time had been concerned mainly with inorganic materials. The study of cellulose and its chemistry led to the understanding that its useful properties were mainly due to its exceedingly large molecular size. Cross and Bevan, and to an even greater extent Staudinger, developed the concept of the macromolecule, which has been basic to plastics development ever since.

Vinyl Polymerization

The next step in the line of plastics development towards the polyolefins was again made quite accidentally. It was found that a coal tar fraction, styrene, was able under very readily attainable conditions to change into a solid substance that also had the characteristics of a giant molecule.

Ostromislensky studied the reaction of styrene with itself and laid the basis for understanding the addition polymerization reaction, which in subsequent years produced a wide variety of valuable new plastics.

The characteristic reacting group in this type of polymerization is a terminal double bond, which is called a vinyl group. A wide variety of materials with such a terminal double bond can be made from coal and petroleum sources. Some of the most important of these raw materials, called monomers in the plastics industry, are vinyl chloride, vinylidene chloride, acrylonitrile, acrylic acid, and substituted acrylic acid esters. These materials, with styrene, gave the plastics industry a plentiful and relatively inexpensive raw materials basis, and led to a rapid expansion of the plastics industry both in volume and variety. At the same time scientific study also expanded.

It was recognized quite early in the study of vinyl polymerization that ethylene was the most basic vinyl monomer, because all of these vinyl materials may be considered substituted ethylenes. It was not, however, possible to polymerize ethylene in the same way as other vinyl monomers because it is a gas and is not dense enough under ordinary conditions to undergo the addition reaction.

Polyethylene

A synthetic material closely resembling linear polyethylene was made and studied just before 1900, but it was produced from diazomethane, an expensive material, so the discovery had no commercial results.

High Pressure Process   The real beginning of polyolefin plastics was the discovery in 1933 by Dr. E. W. Fawcett and Dr. R. O. Gibson of the Imperial Chemical Industries (ICI) laboratories in England of the high pressure process for making polyethylene. This discovery was made incidentally to a general study of the properties of ethylene at high pressure.

After an initial delay due to explosions that occurred when the first experiments were repeated, rapid development of the process took place. The material turned out to be the insulating material needed for the radar defenses that Britain was developing at that time to counter the effect of the "Luftwaffe." In 1938 the first ton was made in pilot plant equipment at Northwich in Cheshire. In 1940 production was 100 tons, and by the end of the war British capacity was 1,500 tons per year. During the war polyethylene production by the ICI process was undertaken by two firms in the U.S.A.

After the war polyethylene production and use increased very rapidly in civilian applications. Communications wire insulation and cable sheathing, injection molding, packaging film, and the squeeze bottle were some of the largest consumers. Production was, however, still limited to the two original producers. In 1952 a federal court ruled that ICI would have to broaden its licensing policy to permit other producers to be established in this country. This resulted in the entry of a number of new producers into the business. Surprisingly the demand for the resin continued to increase, and the greatly increased production capacity was soon all being used.

Low Pressure Processes   In the mid 1950's a great deal of work culminated in the issuance of a series of patents on ethylene polymerization. These were all alike in that they used solid catalysts, operated at relatively low pressure, and produced a polymer that was harder and stronger than ICI polyethylene. While no attempt will be made to follow the exact chronology of these developments, they are so fundamental to the development of polyolefin plastics that a little discussion is needed. The material produced by these processes has been called linear polyethylene for reasons that will become clear in later chapters.

The linear polyethylene processes may be very broadly grouped under three classifications, two of which, the Phillips process and the Standard Oil of Indiana process, are associated with corporations, and the third of which, the Ziegler process, is named for an individual.

The Phillips Process   The Phillips process, developed by the Phillips Petroleum Company, is the leading linear polyethylene process in terms of tonnage in the United States. In this process a chromium oxide catalyst supported on silica or silica-alumina is used. The process is usually practiced in the presence of a volatile hydrocarbon solvent. The finely divided catalyst is suspended in the solvent, and ethylene gas is dissolved in the solvent. As originally practiced the polyethylene produced dissolved in the solvent and was recovered by precipitation after filtration to remove catalyst. More recently a version of this process has been developed, where the polymer is insoluble in the solvent and precipitates out as it is formed. This is often called the "particle form" process. In this form there is no convenient way to remove catalyst residues, so they remain in the polymer. The success of the "particle form" process depends on the use of extremely efficient catalysts which are present in such minute amounts as to be harmless.

The Ziegler Process   The Ziegler process is more widely used outside of the United States than the Phillips process. The polyethylene produced by this process is not quite as stiff and dense as that produced by the Phillips process, but is tougher and has greater stress crack resistance. This process uses a catalyst made from an aluminum alkyl and a titanium chloride. The catalyst is suspended in a hydrocarbon solvent, and the ethylene is dissolved in the solvent. In its original and still usual form the polymer precipitates, but it can be handled in a way so as to form a polymer solution. The great historical importance of the Ziegler process is that the catalysts developed by Ziegler for the polymerization of ethylene were adapted by Natta who used them for the polymerization of propylene.

Standard Oil of Indiana Process   The third group of linear polyethylene patents is called the Standard Oil of Indiana group. While the first patents in this group claimed nickel oxide on an activated carbon carrier, the typical catalyst is now molybdenum oxide on an alumina support, with alkali or alkaline earth metals or hydrides as promoters. While a tremendous amount of scientific work has been put into the development of these catalysts, only a relatively small amount of actual production as yet has resulted. Only two major production facilities for this material exist at present, neither of them in the United States.

Polypropylene

One of the most far reaching developments in polyolefin history was the use of the Ziegler catalysts to polymerize propylene.

This was quite important because by using these catalysts Natta was able to produce a propylene polymer that was entirely different from any that had previously been produced. The polymers of propylene previously made were soft rubbery material, while this was hard and horny, quite similar, in fact, to linear polyethylene. Natta's knowledge of the study of molecular structure by X ray diffraction and other methods enabled him to determine that the remarkable properties of this polymer were due to its extraordinarily regular molecular structure. He called this regular material isotactic polypropylene. We will go into the exact meaning of this term later on in the book.

It had long been known by polymer chemists that many natural high polymers owed their properties to some regularity in their structure. However, attempts to produce a similar material in the laboratory always produced a random or irregular molecule, which often lacked the desirable properties of the natural material.

While isotactic polypropylene has been a successful plastic, it has not created the great interest that some other applications of these stereospecific catalysts have stirred up. Natta's discovery touched off one of the most remarkable bursts of scientific activity the polymer industry has ever seen. Large numbers of catalysts of the same general sort were discovered, and almost every polymerizable material was polymerized by them.

Propylene and other olefins can also be polymerized to the isotactic form by a modified Phillips process and by Standard Oil of Indiana process catalysts.

While it is outside the scope of this book, it should be mentioned that synthetic rubber has been one of the greatest beneficiaries of this discovery, and that industry has been entirely revolutionized by new rubbers based on stereospecific catalysts.

The textile industry has also felt the effect of this discovery; isotactic polypropylene has shown itself to be an excellent textile fiber material and is moving into many fields.

Other Polyolefins

Since the introduction of these three groups of catalysts, the history of polyolefin plastics has been one of tremendous growth in production by the major members of the group polyethylene and polypropylene, and the introduction of several new polymers which have not yet found very large markets, polybutene-1 and most recently poly-4-methylpentene. The major polyolefins themselves have been developed by copolymerization, chemical modifications, cross-linking, and other methods of molecular manipulation, so that one can no longer really identify a simple material in any class but must identify it by properties or end use.

The result is that it is now possible to make polyolefin plastics ranging from soft rubbery materials through hard, heat resistant materials, and from white translucent materials to crystal clear ones. One or another of these is suitable for practically any kind of thermoplastics application.

They compete vigorously in the balance of price and value with other thermoplastics and increasingly with traditional materials of construction.

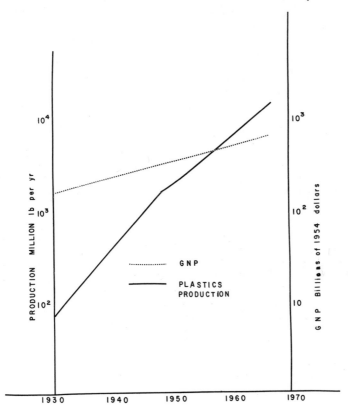

Figure 1.1. Growth of plastics production vs growth of gross national product (G.N.P.).

GROWTH PATTERNS

One of the most remarkable things about plastics, and the polyolefin plastics in particular, is the growth that they have experienced in the past few decades. Plastics production growth in general has far outstripped the rate of growth of the gross national product.

Figure 1.1 shows plastics production in millions of pounds and the gross national product in billions of dollars. The lines shown are the general trend line, disregarding year to year ups and downs.

The polyolefin plastics have, in the past 20 years, been the fastest growing segment of the plastics industry. Figure 1.2 shows the growth lines of polyethylene and polypropylene compared to plastics as a whole.

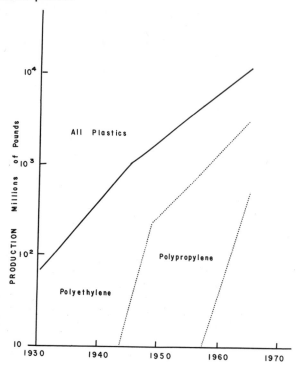

Figure 1.2. Polyolefin plastics growth vs growth of all plastics.

It is quite clear that the polyolefins are growing at a much faster rate than plastics as a whole. While the initial growth rate of polypropylene was not quite as rapid as that of polyethylene, the high initial rate has been sustained up to a higher level of production. Polypropylene is now the fastest growing plastics material and seems likely to reach the billion pound level very soon. While there are several promising new polyolefin plastics, polybutene-1 and poly-4-methylpentene, it does not appear at this point that they will very soon reach high volumes. Polybutene-1 presents some processing problems that appear likely to limit its application, and the cost of the monomer for poly-4-methylpentene appears to be rather high, at least in the near future.

In spite of the lack of any new polyolefin plastics with a growth potential to match that of polyethylene and polypropylene, these alone will keep the polyolefins the fastest growing segment of the plastics industry for some time.

TWO

physical properties

PROPERTIES COMMON TO ALL POLYOLEFIN PLASTICS

Polyolefins are long chain aliphatic hydrocarbons; this means that they belong to the same general class of chemical compounds as paraffin wax. Many of the properties of polyolefin plastics can be understood by analogy with wax, while others are quite different. We will start with the simple wax-like ones.

Water Resistance

Polyolefin plastics are highly water resistant; they absorb practically no water and are quite resistant to the passage of water either in liquid or vapor form. The lack of water absorption means that they do not change dimensions in accordance with changes in atmospheric humidity. They are also very resistant to chemicals in water solution, inorganic salt solutions, acids, and other materials that are highly corrosive to metals but have little or no effect on polyolefins. They are equally resistant to strong alkalis and to hydrofluoric acid which attack glass.

Solvent Resistance

The polyolefin plastics are generally insoluble in solvents at room temperature, although they can be dissolved at elevated temperatures in a variety of solvents, especially the aromatic hydrocarbons. Poly-olefin plastics generally contain a fraction that can be extracted by hydrocarbon solvents at room temperature, and many solvents and oily materials pass through them quite readily.

Gas Barrier Properties

As a class, polyolefin plastics are not very good barriers to oxygen, nitrogen, carbon dioxide, or other gases, but this varies considerably from one polyolefin to another.

STANDARD TEST METHODS

For a detailed study of physical properties we refer to tables of physical properties whose values are the results of numerous tests. While we cannot attempt to describe these tests in detail, a short de-scription of each test will be given, and reference will be made to the appropriate test procedure of the American Society for Testing Materials (ASTM), or other standard reference, for those who need to know the details. A brief comment on the meaning of the test will be made.

Resin Tests

Melt Index ASTM D1238-62T   The polymer is packed into an accurately controlled, heated cylinder which has a small orifice at the bottom. A weighted piston is loaded on top of the polymer mass, forcing a stream of molten polymer out of the orifice. The extrudate is collected over a carefully timed interval and weighed. The weight of polymer extruded in ten minutes is called melt index, abbreviated M.I. This test is a widely used means of classifying polyolefin plas-tics. It is also an indication of how a material will flow in processing, although identical melt index does not necessarily mean identical flow.

Flow Rate D1238-62T   Flow rate is a value similar to melt in-dex but determined under conditions different from the standard melt index conditions. Flow rates are often referred to as melt index, but this results in confusion. For instance, the abbreviation $M.I._{10}$ is used to indicate a flow rate under the same conditions as melt index except that a 10,000 gram weight is substituted for the standard weight. This same designation is used by others to indicate a flow rate at ten times the standard weight, or 21,600 grams. This ASTM procedure lists conditions suitable for determining flow rate for almost any purpose, and provides a positive means of identification for them.

These tests are indications of how the polymer will flow in processing. Using other conditions than standard melt index permits the choice of conditions more suitable to the polymer in question.

Flow Rate Ratio   This is also referred to as Melt Index Ratio (M.I.R.). There is, however, no industry wide standard, so that the exact meaning must be explained with the data to make it meaningful. When the ratio $M.I._{10}/M.I.$ has a high value, it indicates good flow at high shear rates.

Density ASTM D1505-63T   Density is the weight in grams of a cubic centimeter of the material. It is commonly determined by means of a density gradient column. A density gradient column consists of a cylinder of liquid, usually for polyolefins a mixture of an alcohol and water, which has been so constructed as to have a higher proportion of water in the bottom and a higher proportion of alcohol on top with a smooth gradation of concentrations between. The proportions of alcohol and water are chosen to match the density of the sample being tested near the middle of the column. Accurately calibrated glass floats, representing density steps within the range of interest, are then dropped into the column. The floats will drop into the column to the point where the density of the liquid exactly matches the density of the float. The sample to be tested is then dropped in and it will also sink until it reaches the liquid which exactly matches it in density. The location of the sample, and of the float above and below it, is then accurately measured, and the sample density is calculated by interpolation. The temperature of the density gradient column has to be controlled very accurately for good results. The density of a sample of polyolefin reflects its molecular structure, and also the process used in preparing the sample, so that to be meaningful the method of sample preparation must be standardized. Density is widely used to classify polyethylenes, and many properties of polyethylene vary with density. It has little importance on other polyolefins, except simply to show their weight.

Solution Viscosity ASTM D1601-61   This is the viscosity of a dilute solution of the resin in a solvent. Decalin and tetralin are commonly used at a temperature high enough to assure complete solution (130°C is commonly used). There are three ways of reporting this result. One is viscosity ratio or relative viscosity, abbreviated η_{rel}. This is the ratio of the solution viscosity to the viscosity of the pure solvent. The second is logarithmic viscosity number or inherent viscosity (η_{inh}). This is the natural logarithm of the relative viscosity divided by the concentration in grams per 100 ml of solution. The third is limiting viscosity number or intrinsic viscosity, which is the zero concentration intercept of plot of the logarithmic viscosity number against concentration. This number is used as a means of estimating molecular weight, and in conjunction with melt index, may be used to estimate molecular weight distribution.

Environmental Stress Cracking Resistance ASTM D1693   This is sometimes called the bent strip test. A short strip of material is nicked on one side and bent into a "U" shape. The ends of the "U" are held in a channel. A group of 10 strips is placed in one channel, and the assembly is placed in a stress cracking agent (Igepal CO-630 * is standard) at a temperature of 50°C. The samples are observed periodically until they show cracks. The value reported is the time required for half the strips to crack.

This test is a measure of the resistance of the material to attack by the stress crack agent. It is interpreted as an indication of general chemical resistance and general durability of the resin. Since service failures in polyolefin parts frequently occur at well below the normal strength of the resin because of contact with some hostile environment, modifications of this test using different environments are very common.

Tests of Physical Strength

Polyolefins are tested by a variety of strength tests, which are identical with those used for other plastics and also for many other ma-

---

* This is a surface active agent which is a strong detergent.

terials, and should be understood by most readers without explanation. To avoid extending this chapter unduly, these will simply be listed with appropriate references:

Flexural stiffness ASTM D767-58T
Brittleness temperature ASTM D746-59T
Izod impact ASTM D256-56
Shore hardness ASTM D1706-63
Tensile properties (tensile strength, yield point, elongation)
ASTM D638-61T, Appendix
Tensile impact ASTM D1822-61T

Tests on Films

The production of transparent film is such a large part of the polyolefin plastics business that some of the tests used on film should be mentioned.

Haze ASTM D1003-61 This represents the proportion of a transmitted beam of light scattered by a piece of film. It is measured by passing a beam of light through the film and into a light trap which would absorb all of the beam in the absence of the film. The light that is scattered so that it is not absorbed is caught and measured by an integrating sphere photometer. This measurement is compared to the light of the whole beam and reported as percent haze. It represents a milkiness or cloudiness in the film.

Gloss ASTM D523-62T This is a measure of the amount of light reflected from the film when a light beam is directed at the film at an angle. Gloss may be measured at incident angles of 20, 60, and 80° by standard procedure, and 45° is commonly used although not standard. A photo cell measures the beam reflected from the film, and the result is reported in comparison with an arbitrary standard. That is to say, it is not a percentage of anything but merely a level on an arbitrary scale. Gloss represents the visual shininess or sparkle of the film.

Transparency ASTM D1746-62T This measures the scattering of an extremely narrow slit beam of light by the film. It differs from haze mainly in the dimensions of the light beam and its method of measurement. It is reported as the percentage of the incident light that is not scattered, absorbed, or reflected. Since the slit is extremely narrow the value depends on the position of the film, so the film is rotated during measurement and the transmission at different film positions is recorded. Maximum and minimum values are usually reported.

This is a measure of how clearly images can be seen through the film. Evidently very cloudy film cannot have high transparency, but clear film may differ considerably in how much it fuzzes up an image seen through it, and this is what we measure here.

Dart Drop Impact ASTM D1709-62T A sample of film is clamped firmly in a circular holder held horizontally, and a small dart with a spherical head is dropped on the film from a standard height. The dart is arranged so that weights can readily be added to it or taken from it. Drops with varying weights are made until that weight is found which has an equal chance of breaking or not breaking the film.

This is a measure of the ability of the film to withstand the impact loads it will meet in service, such as in a packaging application.

Printability Commercial Standard 227-59, U.S. Dept. of Commerce Most polyolefin films will not accept print in their natural state, so they have to be given a special treatment. The evaluation of the quality of this treatment is the objective of a printability test. The most straightforward, and also most commonly used test for printability is to take a standard ink, apply it to the film, and after it has dried, apply a piece of scotch tape to the ink, and pull the tape off. The percentage of ink retained on the film is reported as percent printable, or percent treatment. Generally 100% ink retention is required.

There are several more sophisticated tests that attempt to get away from the go-no go nature of this test by making indirect tests of properties presumed to be related to printability. Unfortunately we do not know exactly what it is that makes film printable, so these indirect measures do not always correlate exactly with practical printability.

Adhesion Ratio ASTM D2141-63T Pressure sensitive tape is applied to the film under standard conditions and then the force required to peel the tape from the film is measured. This is usually reported as adhesion ratio, which is the ratio of the load required to pull tape from the treated film to that required to pull tape from the untreated film. While this is certainly related to printability, the correlation is often not very good.

Wetting Tension ASTM D2578-67   In this test a series of liquids is made up with graded differences in surface tension. Samples of the series are then swabbed onto the test film, and it is observed if they wet the film, that is to say if they immediately draw up into beads of liquid, or if they stay spread out. When the test liquid that just wets is found, its surface tension is designated as the wetting tension of the film.

This method is widely used as a quality control method because of its speed and ease of use. Within one formulation of film and one treatment method, correlation with printability is good; however the correlation must be established for each kind of film and treatment.

Gas Permeability ASTM D1434-63   A sample of film is clamped into a cell to divide the cell into two chambers. The gas whose permeation is to be determined is placed in one half of the cell. There are two alternative procedures. The gas may be under a pressure higher than atmospheric and the volume passing through measured, or the gas may be at atmospheric pressure, the other side evacuated, and the gas permeating measured by the rise in pressure as gas comes through. With proper precautions both methods give the same results.

When the film is used for packaging, it is important to know how rapidly certain gases, especially carbon dioxide and oxygen will be transmitted. In some cases a degree of permeability is desirable, in others harmful; in either case the amount must be known.

Water Vapor Transmission ASTM E96-53T Proc. E   In this procedure a shallow tray filled with calcium chloride is covered with polyethylene film, and the film is carefully sealed to the tray by the use of a special wax. The tray is weighed, placed in an atmosphere of controlled high humidity, and the weight gain checked periodically.

Polyolefin films are frequently used for the purpose of protecting a material from moisture, so the exact amount transmitted in a given time must be known.

Heat Seal Strength, Commercial Standard 227-59, U.S. Dept. of Commerce   Samples of the film are sealed under standard conditions with a hot bar sealer. The strength of the seal is measured on a tensile tester, and the strength of a continuous piece of the film is also measured. Heat seal strength is reported as percent of film strength.

The usual way of joining two polyolefin films is by means of heat sealing. This means that the quality of seal that can be produced with a given sample of film is important to the user.

Elmendorf Tear Strength ASTM D1922   A special shaped sample of film is clamped into the machine, slit part way through, and then torn apart at the slit by means of a pendulum arrangement. The energy absorbed in tearing is measured by the reduction in pendulum swing.

This is a rather widely used test that has some value in the quality control of film in production. It is not, however, a very useful indication of the strength of film in service.

Blocking   Two sheets of polyolefin film, either directly from a roll where they have been in contact (typically the two sides of a flattened tube), or that have been held together for a time under pressure, are pulled apart in a perpendicular direction. This is accomplished by placing them without parting them between two flat plates, taping one piece of film to one plate and the other to the opposite plate, and measuring the force required to part the plates. There is no standard method for this test, although it is widely used.

Polyolefin film is often used to make bags. If two films have a tendency to cling together, it is difficult to open the bags, so the clinging tendency must be measured.

Other Commonly Used Film Tests   The following tests are of a kind that should be understood from their title:

Coefficient of friction ASTM D1894-61T
Tensile properties ASTM D882-56T

THE POLYOLEFIN PLASTICS PROPERTY SPECTRUM

Some representative physical properties of some of the polyolefins are shown in Table 2.1. These will be discussed in detail below.

TABLE 2.1. Physical Properties of Polyolefin Plastics

Property	Polyethylene			Polypropylene			Poly-butene-1	Poly-4-methyl-pentene	EVA copolymer	Ionomer
	Low Den.	Med. Den.	Linear	Homopolymer	Copolymer	Impact				
Density gm/cc	.910-.925	.926-.940	.941-.965	.902-.906	.89-.905	.90-.91	.910-.915	.83	.92-.95	.935-.956
Tensile strength 1000 psi	1-2.3	1.2-3.5	3.1-5.5	4.3-5.5	2.9-4.5	2.8-4.4	3.8-4.0	4.0	1.0-2.5	3.5-5.5
Elongation %	90-800	50-600	50-1000	200-700	200-700	350-500	300-380	15	300-700	300-500
Tensile modulus 10^5 psi	.14-.38	.25-.55	.6-1.8	1.6-2.5	1.0-1.7	1.0-1.7	.26	2.1	.02-.12	.28-.60
Izod impact ft lb/in. notch	N.B.	0.5-16.0	0.8-20.0	.5-2.0	1.1-20.0	1.7	NB	.08	NB	5.7-14.6
Flex modulus 10^5 psi	.08-.60	.61-1.15	1.0-1.6	2.3-2.7	1.25-2.0	—	.49	—	—	—
Thermal conductivity cal/cm²/sec/°C/cm x 10^4	8.0	8.0-10.0	11-12.4	2.8	2.0-4.0	3.0-4.0	—	4.0	—	5.8
Specific heat cal/gm/°C	.55	.55	.55	.46	.50	.50	.45	.52	.55	.55
Thermal expansion in./in./°F x 10^5	10-20	14-16	11-13	5.8-10	8-9.5	6-8.5	15	11.7	16-20	10-12
Heat deflection temperature °F 264 psi	90-105	105-120	110-130	125-140	125-140	120-135	130-140	—	93	
66 psi	100-121	120-165	140-190	200-230	185-230	160-200	215-235	—	140-147	108-113

Density

The polyolefins are all light weight materials, none having a density above that of water. Poly-4-methylpentene (TPX) is the lightest and linear polyethylene the heaviest. In the overall group, density has little relationship to other physical properties, but within the polyethylenes there is a close relationship between density and other properties. Since the polyethylenes very nearly span the range of the polyolefins in many properties, it is useful to consider all the polyolefins in relation to the polyethylene spectrum.

As polyethylene density increases, tensile strength, stiffness, heat resistance, yield strength, and hardness all increase. Permeability, stress crack resistance, impact strength, and tear strength decrease at the same time (see Figure 2.1).

Increasing Density

Increases	Decreases
Stiffness	Permeability
Tensile Strength	Stress Crack resistance
Yield Strength	
Heat Resistance	Impact Resistance
Hardness	Tear Strength

Figure 2.1. Effect of density on properties of polyethylene.

Tensile Strength

In tensile strength all of the other polyolefins fall within the polyethylene spectrum with polypropylene, poly-4-methylpentene, and the ionomers in the high density polyethylene range, and EVA copolymer in the low density range.

Stiffness

Tensile modulus, however, shows a different picture, and we see that unmodified polypropylene and poly-4-methylpentene are both stiffer materials than linear polyethylene, while the EVA copolymer may be very considerably less stiff than low density polyethylene. In the copolymer, stiffness depends on comonomer content, with high co-monomer content giving more flexible materials. While no figures are given for the other copolymers of ethylene with polar monomers, such as the acrylates, these too are less stiff materials whose properties can be best understood as extensions of the polyethylene property spectrum on the low density side.

Heat Resistance

When heat deflection temperature is considered, an even more marked extension of the polyethylene spectrum can be observed. All of the polypropylenes, polybutene-1 and poly-4-methylpentene, are more heat resistant than the most heat resistant linear polyethylene. This extension of the spectrum is particularly important because, if we consider the 66 psi distortion temperature, we see that this goes above the boiling point of water on these materials. Since many plastics applications involve temperatures at or near the boiling point of water, it can be seen that a really useful extension of polyolefin applications results from this improved heat resistance. The EVA copolymer figures show that while its stiffness is below that of low density polyethylene, its 66 psi heat distortion temperature falls in the range of high density polyethylene. This means that it is a flexible but relatively heat resistant material. Polybutene-1 has stiffness in the low density polyethylene range, and higher heat distortion temperature than low density polyethylene. This useful combination of properties is shared by some of the other ethylene polar copolymers as well.

Elongation

The wide ranges given for the elongations of most of the materials shown result from the phenomenon of cold draw. Cold draw is very important in many of the polyolefin plastics processing techniques where the processing consists in part of drawing the material at a temperature well below its melting point. These elongations are similar in size to the elongations shown by some rubbers but are entirely different in nature. The rubber elongation is entirely reversible, and the plastic elongation is permanent and irreversible in most cases. The polar copolymers may have a reversible elongation, which gives them a rubbery character, and to some degree the ionomers also have this nature. At this time we cannot judge whether the low elongation of poly-4-methylpentene is characteristic of the entire line of such polymers, or if it is only a property of the first resin of this class that has been produced.

In order to understand the importance of the high elongations of polyolefins in their end use, consideration of a typical polyolefin plastic stress-strain curve is useful.

Figure 2.2 shows such a curve. Numerical values for stress have been omitted because these differ considerably between polyolefins. Numerical values for strain also differ considerably from one polyolefin to another, but numbers have been put in for purposes of discussion.

When the typical polyolefin is first loaded, it responds with a nearly straight line stress-strain relation. However, this begins to

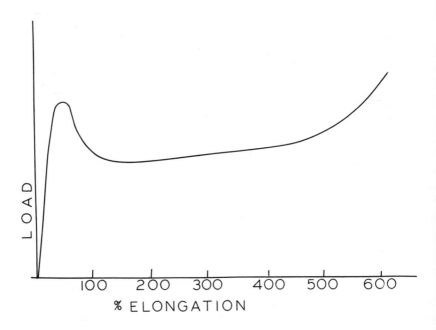

Figure 2.2. Typical polyolefin stress-strain curve.

curve in the larger strain direction after about 2-5% elongation. This curve continues to flatten out until somewhere in the 15-25% elongation region, then strain will continue without added stress. This is called the yield point. From this point onward, elongation continues at constant or even slightly diminished stress. This is the cold draw region of the curve. After several hundred percent cold draw elongation, the stress required begins a slow rise, which may go well above the yield point, if rupture does not occur until 800 or 900 percent, elongation.

To understand the importance of this stress-strain behavior in practical use, let's take a sample that has reached 800% elongation at a stress of 4000 psi based on its original cross section. Remember that this elongation is permanent, so we can remove the sample from the tester and measure its cross section. It will, of course, be $\frac{1}{8}$ of its original cross section. If we then calculate its strength based on this new cross section, it will come out 4000 $\times$ 8 or 32,000 psi. This means that we can make polyolefin plastics much stronger simply by stretching them. Polyolefin monofilament, oriented film, and fiber technologies are all based on this simple fact.

The wide range in elongation reported for each polyolefin results from the fact that while each will follow a characteristic curve, similar to Figure 2.2, rupture of the sample will occur at different distances along the curve. One of the things that determines where it will break is melt index. High melt index resins of any kind tend to break at low elongation, while low melt index resins will carry along to higher elongations. Rate of strain is also very important, because high rates of strain will reduce elongation, particularly with the stiffer materials. While the quoted elongations are all at 73°F, temperature is also very important, the higher temperatures giving greater elongations. Method of sample preparation makes a great difference in elongation. Injection molded samples will have a much lower elongation than an extruded strand or a compression molded piece of the same resin. Samples cooled very rapidly will generally elongate more than slowly cooled samples.

Izod Impact

The impact strength of polyolefin plastics varies a great deal. Table 2.1 shows that this variation is not so much between resin types as within types. Certain polyolefins, low density polyethylene and polar copolymers do not break in the Izod impact test; they just bend, so no figures can be given. Even the lowest numbers given represent quite respectable impact values. There are many usable plastics with Izod impact values of only a few hundredths of a ft lb per inch. This means that 0.5 ft lb per inch is really quite impact resistant. On the other end of the scale, the very high impact strengths of some linear polyethylenes and polypropylene copolymers represent formulations designed to optimize these properties.

In the case of linear polyethylene, high impact strength is obtained by copolymerization with higher alpha olefins. These have not been specifically mentioned before because they form a continuous property spectrum with the homopolymers. Linear polyethylene with a density below about .955 is produced by copolymerization. The high impact strength of some polypropylene is also produced by copolymerization, but, in this case, the comonomer is usually ethylene.

Flexural Modulus

This is just another measure of stiffness, it is generally somewhat higher than tensile modulus, and varies in a similar manner. Theoretically they should be the same but the different method of test gives slightly different values.

Thermal Conductivity

The difference in conductivity is related to the basic raw material. Polyethylenes generally have higher conductivities than polymers of other olefins; and among polyethylenes conductivity increases with density. This difference is important in processing because most processing methods involve putting heat into the plastic and then taking it out again. When this heat transfer involves conduction, it is easier with a resin of higher thermal conductivity. This gives linear polyethylene a considerable advantage over polypropylene in processes such as thermoforming, bottle blowing, and injection molding. Cycle time can be shorter with polyethylene because heat transfer is faster.

The thermal conductivity of all polyolefin plastics is very low compared to metals, and many other materials. This means that they have some degree of thermal insulating value. Polyolefin objects that are regularly handled in use will be pleasant to touch, because, whether they are warm or cold, they will not transfer heat to or from the hands rapidly.

Specific Heat

Speed of heating and cooling depends not only on thermal conductivity but also on specific heat. The differences in specific heat is not very great between polyolefin plastics. Polypropylene has a little advantage over polyethylene in this respect, but it generally does not compensate for the difference in thermal conductivity. It would be significant only in case the limiting factor in a production process was the ability of the machine to handle the heating or cooling load.

Thermal Expansion

Polyolefin plastics have high thermal expansion compared to metal and other construction materials. This must be taken into consideration when they are used in some product along with other materials. If polyolefins are rigidly fastened to some material with lower thermal expansion, like steel for instance, excessive stresses could be built up when the temperature changes. This is not important with flexible polyolefins, like low density polyethylene or polar copolymers, but can be serious with the stiffer materials, especially on large size parts. Methods of joining should provide flexibility to compensate for the expansion differences.

Polyolefin Properties Related to Melt Index

Melt index is brought up at this time in relation to its influence on physical properties. In many processing methods it is convenient to have a resin that flows very readily. This means a high melt index resin. While it is, of course, necessary to use a melt index high enough to make the process practicable, the use of high melt index materials entails certain penalties in other physical properties.

The most striking melt index dependent property is environmental stress crack resistance, which drops very sharply as melt index is increased. This is, in the strictest sense, a polyethylene property, for the other polyolefins do not have the same susceptibility to Igepal, the standard stress cracking reagent. The other polyolefins, however, all have some reagents, or environmental materials that attack them and cause premature failure, and their susceptibility to such failure is greater for high flow materials. This can be interpreted very generally in terms of service life and general resistance to deterioration by outside influences. Resistance to aging can, of course, be improved sharply by certain additives which protect against specific dangers, such as oxidation or ultraviolet irradiation, but along with these, there is also a component related to flow.

Higher flow materials within any group also show some loss in physical properties such as tensile strength, but this is only true of extreme differences, and in some cases, such as in polypropylene, there may even be higher tensiles with higher melt index. Elongation, however, is much more flow dependent, and the technologies that make use of the strength increasing effect of high elongation, are effective mainly on relatively low melt index polyolefin plastics.

Impact strength generally is lower in high melt index materials. The flow properties of a polyolefin plastic are related to melt index but are not entirely specified by it. In particular, melt index cannot be compared between different types of polyolefin plastics, and even within resins of the same class, the flow behavior of two resins with the same melt index may differ appreciably.

RELATION OF PHYSICAL PROPERTIES TO MOLECULAR WEIGHT DISTRIBUTION

The effect of some of the details of molecular structure on polymer properties will be discussed in the next chapter where the structure is explained. Here we are concerned with molecular weight and molecular weight distribution.

The properties of all high polymers depend on the fact that they do have extremely high molecular weights, and the level of molecular weight within this range has an important influence on the level of certain properties. The commercial polyolefins are all polydisperse materials, which means that any polyolefin sample consists of molecules of many different molecular weights.

Molecular Weight Averages

When we speak of the molecular weight of any given sample, we must therefore speak of an average molecular weight. Two kinds of averages are commonly quoted, these are Number Average M_n or $\bar{N}$ and Weight Average M_w or $\bar{W}$. The number average is the simple average used for most purposes and is determined by weighing the sample, going through some procedure that counts the number of molecules, and dividing the total weight by the total number of molecules. Many of the effects of molecular weight depend disproportionately on the larger molecules in the mixture, so the weight average is used to emphasize the importance of the large molecules. This average consists of the weight of the molecules of each size, multiplied by their molecular weight, and the sum of these products for all the sizes represented is divided by the total number of molecules.

Dispersivity Ratio

These two averages will be identical if the material is all of one size, but as soon as there is a range of sizes, M_w becomes larger than M_n.

This gives a convenient index in the width of the molecular weight distribution M_w/M_n. This is called the dispersivity ratio.

Molecular Weight Distribution Curve

In addition to these averages and the ratio, it is useful to know the entire molecular weight distribution. This is conveniently represented in the form of a molecular weight distribution curve. An example of such a curve is given in Figure 2.3. In this curve the molecular weight is shown across the base of the curve, while the height of the curve shows the amount of material of the corresponding molecular weight.

Until very recently the determination of a molecular weight distribution curve was a lengthy and laborious undertaking which required fractionating the sample into a number of fractions of comparatively narrow molecular weight distribution, and then determining the amount and molecular weight of each fraction.

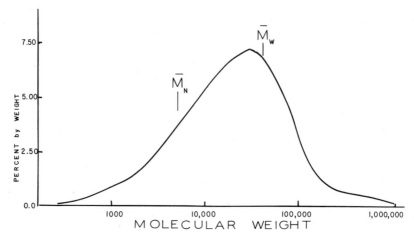

Figure 2.3. Typical polyolefin molecular weight distribution curve.

Gel Permeation Chromatography

In recent years, however, the technique of gel permeation chromatography has been developed and incorporated into an automatic machine which, when properly calibrated for the resin in question, can determine all the necessary information in a few hours. A digital computer is then used to convert this information into a complete molecular weight distribution curve with calculation of any desired molecular weight averages, dispersivity ratios, etc. This has proved to be a valuable tool in resin development work, and also permits precise quality control work.

Gel permeation chromatography also makes it possible to follow the changes in molecular size occurring during processing or use, to detect degradation, or to predict property changes.

This technique is so new that the influence of the details of the molecular weight distribution curve on the properties of the plastic is still closely withheld proprietary information. However, it can be said that the curves found for competitive polyolefin plastics of the same end use are generally closely similar; and within any one polyolefin, if the molecular weight distribution curve of a product is matched, the match will have very nearly the same processing and end use properties.

Interpretation of Distribution Curves

A few general statements may be made to illustrate the value of these curves.

In the case of polyethylene a broad molecular weight distribution has several advantages over narrow. In processing it will have greater shear sensitivity of melt flow. That is to say, at low shear stresses it will flow little, but as shear stress is increased, shear rate will increase a disproportionate amount. This is useful in blow molding, where low parison sag (low shear rate) may be coupled with easy flow through the die (high shear rate).

However, some disadvantages accompany broad distribution. The physical properties will not be quite as good as a material of similar melt index but narrower distribution. When the material is used for injection molding, warpage is more severe. Similar effects are found with other polyolefins.

TEMPERATURE DEPENDENCE OF PHYSICAL PROPERTIES

Up to this point we have mainly discussed room temperature physical properties, but the physical properties of all polyolefins are dependent to a great degree on temperature.

Polyethylene

To illustrate this, some properties of polyethylene are shown in Figure 2.4 plotted against temperature. In these curves the three types represent density ranges.

Type 1	Low density	.910-.925
Type 2	Medium density	.925-.940
Type 3	High density	.940-.960

It can be seen that yield tensile strength, ultimate tensile strength, and modulus of elasticity, are all high at low temperature and drop sharply as the temperature increases. Elongation is quite different and rises to a maximum, which is at a higher temperature with the higher density resin, and is also much more marked with Type 1.

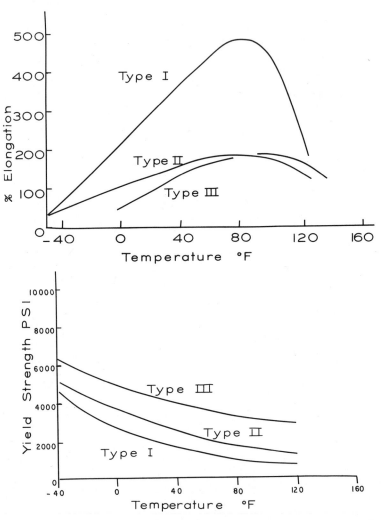

Figure 2.4. Temperature dependence of selected physical properties of poly-ethylene.

This kind of behavior is characteristic of all thermoplastic materials and is the main factor limiting their applications at extreme temperature.

Comparison with Vinyl

The polyolefins do not show as rapid a change in properties with temperature as do many other thermoplastics. Table 2.2 compares

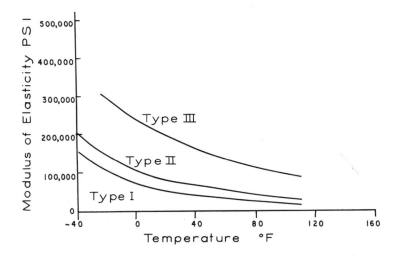

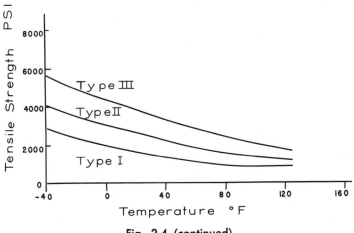

Fig. 2.4 (continued)

low density polyethylene and some ethylene copolymers with a typical vinyl resin.

In order to make the comparison more convenient, a commercial vinyl compound was selected which had approximately the same room temperature stiffness as the ethylene vinyl acetate copolymer (EVA), and the ethylene ethyl acrylate copolymer (EEA) available.

The vinyl compound has nearly the same impact strength at room temperature as the polyolefins, but at $-30°C$ the vinyl has lost prac-

TABLE 2.2. Physical Properties of Some Flexible Polyolefin Plastics Compared to a Flexible Vinyl.

Property	°C	EVA	EEA	LDPE	Vinyl
Tensile impact ft lb/sq in.[1]	23	690	500	388	425
	−30	260	390	175	25
Brittleness index, 50% failure °C [2]		−100°	−100°	−80°	−15°
Stiffness 1000 psi [3]	70	1.2	.4	3.0	.45
	60	1.7	.6	4.0	.6
	50	2.4	1.0	6.5	.9
	40	3.4	1.5	10.0	1.8
	25	5.1	4.5	18.0	4.5
	0	11.0	8.0	35.0	45.0
	−25	64.0	23.0	70.0	200.0
	−50	186.0	155.0	180.0	400.0

[1] ASTM D1822.
[2] ASTM D746.
[3] 1% Secant modulus.

tically all its impact strength, while the polyolefins retain a great deal of theirs. The ethylene ethyl acrylate copolymer, in particular, retains a remarkable amount of impact strength at this low temperature. This is typical of copolymers of ethylene and the various acrylate monomers, and makes them very useful for low temperature applications.

The brittleness index, which is the temperature at which half the samples fail under impact, tells a similar story. The polyolefins resist breakage at extremely low temperatures, while the vinyl becomes brittle at moderately low temperature.

The stiffness change with temperature also shows the superiority of the polyolefins in comparison with the vinyl. The EVA copolymer, which closely matches the stiffness of the vinyl at low temperature, retains more stiffness at high temperature and does not increase stiffness as much as the vinyl at low temperature. The EEA copolymer softens about as much at high temperature but stiffens much less at low temperature than the vinyl. The low density polyethylene is stiffer at high temperature but more flexible at low temperature than the vinyl.

Other Polyolefins

The other polyolefins show generally similar behavior with temperature changes, all of them show wide, usable temperature ranges in comparison with other thermoplastics. Unmodified polypropylene becomes brittle at moderately low temperatures, and this has been a serious limitation on its use. The great expansion in polypropylene applications has paralleled the development of impact resistant grades, especially copolymers with ethylene. Figure 2.5 shows the relationship of tensile impact strength and temperature for several polypropylenes.

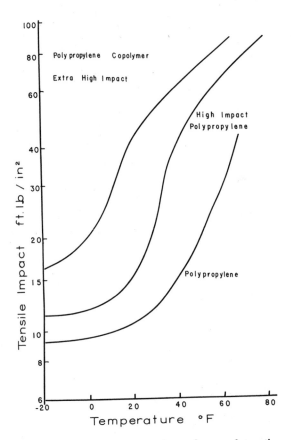

Figure 2.5. Temperature dependence of tensile impact of several types of polypropylene.

CRYSTALLINITY

The relationship between the density of polyethylene and its physical properties was mentioned earlier without detailing the reason for the relationship.

The reason why density plays such an important part in polyethylene properties is that it is a measure of crystallinity. Polyethylene crystals are more dense than amorphous polyethylene. Therefore, the density of the aggregate reflects the degree of crystallinity. The other polyolefins have lower crystal densities than polyethylene, so have lower mass densities, even at high degrees of crystallinity.

It would seem more logical, therefore, to report the percent crystallinity rather than density, but this is not readily done. Crystallinity has been measured by X ray diffraction, by infrared absorption, and by differential thermal analysis (DTA), but these different methods do not measure quite the same quality. Therefore, there is really no generally accepted definition or reliably comparable data available on crystallinity.

A complicating factor in the relationship of physical properties to crystallinity is that the size of the crystalline aggregates, as well as the total amount of crystallinity affects the physical properties. Large crystalline aggregates stiffen the polymer and cause it to become brittle. This is one reason for the loss of flexibility on aging. Time, particularly at elevated temperature, causes an increase in size of the crystalline aggregates, as well as a gradual increase in total crystallinity.

One of the reasons why high molecular weight polyolefins show superior aging characteristics is the tendency for very long chains to limit crystallinity and crystal size.

Crystallinity is responsible for much of the tensile strength of polyolefins. The bonds between molecules are very weak. When the resin crystallizes, the molecules conform more closely, so that the weak intermolecular forces have a greater chance to become effective, and this is what gives the plastic its strength.

The nature and configuration of the polyolefin crystals will be discussed in the next chapter.

THREE

chemistry of polyolefins

VINYL POLYMERIZATION

The basic reaction involved in the manufacture of polyolefins is the same one that is used in the manufacture of all the other high volume thermoplastics. It is addition polymerization based on vinyl unsaturation. This may be represented in simplified form as:

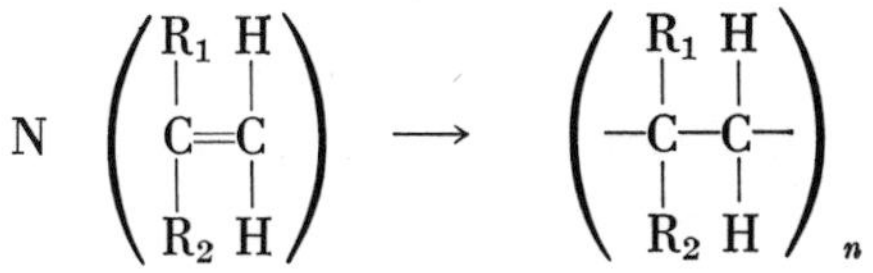

$$N \begin{pmatrix} R_1 & H \\ | & | \\ C\!=\!C \\ | & | \\ R_2 & H \end{pmatrix} \longrightarrow \begin{pmatrix} R_1 & H \\ | & | \\ -C\!-\!C\!- \\ | & | \\ R_2 & H \end{pmatrix}_n$$

In the case of polyolefins R_1 is hydrogen and R_2 is hydrogen or a hydrocarbon group. The R_2 group and the complete formula for each commonly used monomer are shown in Table 3.1.

These materials are polymerized alone, and also copolymerized with each other. Other materials used as comonomers have the same reactive vinyl group and differ only in the nature of R_2. Some of the most common are shown in Table 3.2.

The different monomers affect the nature of the polymer produced, and because of their own different physical properties, they influence the conditions under which the reaction takes place, but they do not fundamentally affect the polymerization reaction itself. We will

33

TABLE 3.I.   The Principal Olefin Monomers

R_2	Chemical Formula	Olefin Name
—H	$\begin{array}{c} H \quad\; H \\ | \quad\;\; | \\ C = C \\ | \quad\;\; | \\ H \quad\; H \end{array}$	Ethylene
—CH_3	$\begin{array}{c} H \quad\; H \\ | \quad\;\; | \\ C = C \\ | \quad\;\; | \\ CH_3 \; H \end{array}$	Propylene
—$C_2 H_5$	$\begin{array}{c} H \quad\; H \\ | \quad\;\; | \\ C = C \\ | \quad\;\; | \\ C_2 H_5 \, H \end{array}$	Butene-1
$\begin{array}{c} H \; H \\ | \; | \\ -C-C-CH_3 \\ | \; | \\ H \; C \\ | \\ H_3 \end{array}$	$\begin{array}{c} H \quad\; H \\ | \quad\;\; | \\ C = C \\ | \quad\;\; | \\ H_2 \, C \quad H \\ | \\ H-C-CH_3 \\ | \\ CH_3 \end{array}$	4-Methylpentene

therefore discuss the reaction just in terms of ethylene, understanding that the others react the same way. In order to get some idea of the nature of this reaction, we need to look at the carbon atom itself and see how it produces the coordinate bonds which are the fundamental links in all polymers.

The Co-ordinate Bond of the Carbon Atom

The carbon atom has in its outer shells four electrons which are capable of forming bonds with other carbon atoms or with atoms of other kinds. These four electrons are equal in reactivity and occupy elliptical orbitals about the nucleus. Since electrons are repulsed from each other by electrostatic forces, these orbitals locate

TABLE 3.2. Common Comonomers Used with Olefins

R_2	Formula	Name
$-C_4H_9$	H H | | C = C | | C_4H_9 H	1-Hexene
$-O-C-CH_3$ ‖ O	H H | | C = C | | O H | O=C$-CH_3$	Vinyl acetate
$O=C-O-CH_3$	H H | | C = C | H O=C$-O-CH_3$	Methyl acrylate
O ‖ $-C-OH$	H H | | C = C | H O=C$-OH$	Acrylic acid

themselves so as to be as far apart from each other as possible, yet
still include the nucleus. This mutual repulsion causes the four orbitals to have axes of symmetry that point in the direction of the corners of a regular tetrahedron with the nucleus in the center. Figure
3.1 is a rough representation of these orbitals.

When carbon forms a coordinate bond, it shares one of these electron orbitals with an electron from the atom bonded. Ethane, the
saturated hydrocarbon corresponding to ethylene, may be represented as shown in Figure 3.2.

There are now two electrons in each orbital, and the nucleus to
which the electron is attached is bonded to the carbon.

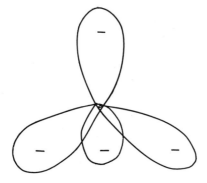

Figure 3.1. Electron orbitals of the carbon atom.

Under certain conditions two carbon atoms may form what is called a double bond, in which four electrons are shared between the two carbons. It can be seen that if we would try to get two orbitals between the atoms we would severely distort their normal positions. This causes one electron from each atom to enter a different sort of orbital, called a pi orbital, much nearer the nucleus. The three remaining normal orbitals, freed of the electrostatic repulsion of the fourth electron, now take a planar position, much like the petals of a perfectly flat flower, while the pi orbital lies above and below this

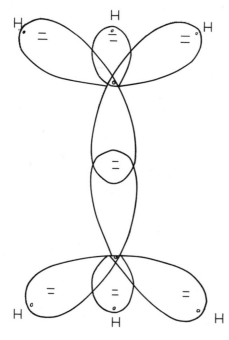

Figure 3.2. Electron orbitals of ethane.

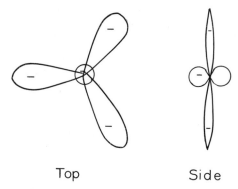

Top   Side

Figure 3.3. Pi orbitals of carbon atom.

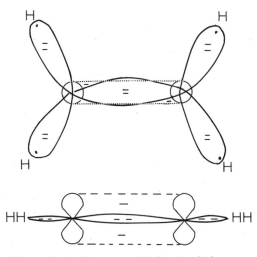

Figure 3.4. Electron orbitals of ethylene.

plane, perpendicular to the plane. This is difficult to represent by a single diagram, so Figure 3.3 shows two views of the atom, one perpendicular to, and one parallel to the plane of the three orbitals.

Notice that the pi orbital has two lobes, one above and one below the plane of the normal orbitals, but one electron occupies both lobes. The double bond is formed by having two electrons occupy one normal orbital, and two others the pi orbitals of both atoms. Figure 3.4 represents ethylene.

It can now be understood that if we bring this in contact with some material that can immobilize or react with one of the electrons in the pi orbital, there will be an unpaired electron available in the molecule. This electron can then pair with the pi electron in another ethylene molecule, making a normal orbital and joining the molecules but, of course, producing a new unpaired electron and so on. This reaction continues because the normal orbital is a condition of lower energy than the pi orbital, so energy is released, driving the reaction.

The two methods of manufacturing polyolefins differ only in the way in which the electron is attacked.

Free Radical Polymerization

Free radical polymerization consists of three basic steps: initiation, propagation, and termination. Chain transfer also takes place and modifies the polymer produced. These reactions are shown in Figure 3.5.

Initiation

$ROOR \longrightarrow 2RO^*$
$RO^* + CH_2 = CH_2 \longrightarrow ROCH_2 - CH_2^*$

Propagation

$ROCH_2 - CH_2^* + N (CH_2 = CH_2) \longrightarrow$
$RO(CH_2 - CH_2)_n - CH_2 CH_2^*$

Termination
    Coupling
$2RO(CH_2 - CH_2)_n - CH_2 CH_2^* \longrightarrow$
$RO(CH_2 - CH_2)_n - (CH_2 \cdot CH_2)_n CH_2 - CH_2OR$

Disproportionation

or

$\longrightarrow$

$RO(CH_2 - CH_2)_n CH = CH_2 + RO(CH_2 - CH_2)_n - CH_2CH_3$

Chain Transfer

$RO - CH_2CH_2^* + HX \longrightarrow ROCH_2 CH_3 + X^*$
$X^* + CH_2 = CH_2 \longrightarrow XCH_2CH_2^*$

* Asterisks indicate free radicals.

Figure 3.5. Reactions of free radical polymerization.

Initiation   In the initiation step an unstable molecule is introduced, which decomposes to produce fragments which have an active unpaired electron. These are called free radicals. The free radical pairs with one pi electron and starts the chain reaction previously described.

By far the most commonly used free radical source is a peroxide. A peroxide is inherently unstable, and undergoes decomposition quite rapidly as the temperature rises.

Table 3.3 shows some peroxides and other unstable molecules that can be used as initiators for free radical polymerization.

TABLE 3.3.   Initiators for Free Radical Polymerization

Name	Formula
Benzoyl peroxide	$\langle\bigcirc\rangle\!-\!\overset{\overset{\text{O}}{\|}}{\text{C}}\!-\!\text{O}\!-\!\text{O}\!-\!\overset{\overset{\text{O}}{\|}}{\text{C}}\!-\!\langle\bigcirc\rangle$
Acetyl peroxide	$\text{CH}_3\!-\!\overset{\overset{\text{O}}{\|}}{\text{C}}\!-\!\text{O}\!-\!\text{O}\!-\!\overset{\overset{\text{O}}{\|}}{\text{C}}\!-\!\text{CH}_3$
Di-*tert*-butyl peroxide	$\begin{array}{c}\text{CH}_3 \qquad\qquad \text{CH}_3\\ \text{CH}_3\!-\!\text{C}\!-\!\text{O}\!-\!\text{O}\!-\!\text{C}\!-\!\text{CH}_3\\ \text{CH}_3 \qquad\qquad \text{CH}_3\end{array}$
Decanoyl peroxide	$\text{C}_9\text{H}_{19}\!-\!\text{C}\!-\!\text{O}\!-\!\text{O}\!-\!\text{C}\!-\!\text{C}_9\text{H}_{19}$
Lauroyl peroxide	$\text{C}_{11}\text{H}_{23}\!-\!\text{C}\!-\!\text{O}\!-\!\text{O}\!-\!\text{C}\!-\!\text{C}_{11}\text{H}_{23}$
Azobisisobutyro nitrile	$\begin{array}{c}\text{CH}_3 \qquad\qquad \text{CH}_3\\ \text{CH}_3\!-\!\text{C}\!-\!\text{N}\!=\!\text{N}\!-\!\text{C}\!-\!\text{CH}_3\\ \text{CH}_3 \qquad\qquad \text{CH}_3\end{array}$

The initiator, while it is commonly called a catalyst, is not a true catalyst because it enters into, and is consumed in the reaction. It is therefore preferable to call these substances initiators. The first polyethylene made by ICI was oxygen initiated. Oxygen is not, of itself, a free radical former; however, under reaction conditions it reacts with ethylene to form hydroperoxides which then decompose to form free radicals. The oxygen initiated reaction proved difficult to control, and at present most producers use free radical forming organic compounds as initiators.

The choice of initiator depends on several factors. In the first place a material of reasonable room temperature stability is desirable, so as not to complicate the handling of the material. The second important factor is that the material should decompose quickly at the reaction temperature, so as not to delay the reaction. Table 3.4 lists some initiators and their half life at various temperatures.

TABLE 3.4. Half Life of Organic Peroxides (hours)

Peroxide	30	40	50	60	70	80	90	100	110	120	130	140	150
						Temperature °C							
Diisopropyl peroxy-carbonate	19	6.2	2.2	.84	.33	.14							
tert-Butyl peroxypivalate			20	5.1	1.5	.47	.16						
Lauroyl peroxide				13	3.4	.93	.30	.09					
Decanoyl peroxide				13	3.4	.93	.29	.07					
Acetyl peroxide				32	8.0	2.1	.57	.16	.05				
Benzoyl peroxide				45	13	3.8	1.2	.40	.14	.05			
tert-Butyl peroxybenzoate								18	5.4	1.7	.55	.19	.07
tert-Butyl peroxide										21	6.4	2.2	.85

You will observe that in order to get a short half life at fairly low reaction temperatures, it is necessary to accept a lower half life at storage temperatures. Since reaction temperature has an important influence on the nature of the polymer produced, different initiators are generally used for different kinds of resin. The very active initiators which are needed for low temperature reactions are used only when needed, while for the higher temperature reactions, the more stable initiators, which do not need special storage and handling, are used. Other considerations are cost and efficiency, that is its ability to produce free radicals without undergoing undesirable side reactions which will not initiate polymerization or which will produce off odors or colors. Since the initiator residue becomes a part of the polymer molecule, which means that it will be present in the finished resin, it is necessary that this residue have no harmful properties.

Because of the high molecular weight of the product, a small amount of initiator produces a large amount of resin. In order to facilitate feeding small amounts of material, and also in order to handle a less unstable initiator mixture, it is common practice to dilute the initiator before feeding it to the reactor. Mineral oil is a common diluent, but several other solvents are also used. An initiator diluent must be chosen carefully to avoid harmful residues in the polymer or modification of the reaction. The use of a solvent makes it possible to feed solid initiators in liquid form. This is important because the initiator must be fed to the reactor, which is at a very high pressure. Liquid pumps do this readily, but there is no way to do it with a solid.

Propagation   The propagation reaction consists of the initial free radical joining with a series of ethylene molecules in rapid succession. This is a very fast reaction and several thousand ethylene molecules will be linked up in a fraction of a second until the reaction is stopped by either coupling, disproportionation, or chain transfer.

Termination   Two termination reactions result from the collision of two free radicals or growing chains. In the case of coupling the two chains merely grow together, thereby extinguishing both free radicals. In the case of disproportionation one free radical abstracts a hydrogen atom from the other, thereby becoming saturated and inactive, while the other free radical becomes an unsaturated hydrocarbon, but no longer a free radical and may enter another growing chain. This reaction can produce long chain branching in the polymer because the first formed polymer chain will appear as a side branch on the polymer formed in the second reaction.

Growing free radicals can also be terminated by a reaction that does not extinguish the free radical but merely removes it from the one growing chain and allows it to start another. This reaction is called chain transfer. The chain transfer agent is a molecule with an active hydrogen atom. The free radical abstracts the active hydrogen from the chain transfer agent, thereby becoming saturated and inactive, but the removal of the hydrogen in this case turns the transfer agent into a free radical which proceeds to grow another chain. It is evident that the use of chain transfer agents is a means of controlling polymer chain length.

The chain transfer agent is, like the initiator, consumed in the reaction and becomes a part of the finished polymer molecule. When the transfer agent is a low molecular weight hydrocarbon, it is indistinguishable from polymerized ethylene. This is a means of introducing very small amounts of material that would not ordinarily polymerize into polyethylene, if desired. It is also a way in which small amounts of unwanted atoms can get into the polymer.

Stereospecific Catalysts

As mentioned earlier, polyolefins can also be produced by an entirely different kind of initiator. These are solid materials and true catalysts in the sense that they are not consumed in the reaction. The initiation reaction in this case occurs on the catalyst surface where an active site is produced during catalyst preparation. This active site, in the presence of monomer, grows a polymer molecule, the equivalent of the propagation reaction. This propagation reaction is, however, much slower than that of the free radical method, and the polymer molecule may in some cases take an hour or more to grow. The termination reaction in this case consists merely of the release of the molecule from the active site by thermodynamic forces, leaving the active site free to start growing another molecule of polymer. The active site will continue to grow polymer until destroyed by a catalyst poison, or removed from the source of monomer.

Ziegler Catalysts   A typical Ziegler catalyst is made by mixing titanium tetrachloride with aluminum trimethyl. The exact reaction is not fully understood, but the mixture certainly changes its nature entirely, and the catalyst formed in no way resembles the original reactants. Some other Ziegler catalysts are shown in Table 3.5.

TABLE 3.5.   Some Typical Ziegler Catalysts for Polymerization of Olefins

Name	Formula	CoCatalyst	Monomer
Titanium tetrachloride	$TiCl_4$	$Al(Et)_3$	Ethylene
Titanium trichloride	$TiCl_3$	$Al(Et)_3$	Propylene
Vanadium oxychloride	$VO\ Cl_3$	$Al(Hexyl)_3$	Ethylene-propylene

The exact mechanism of these catalysts is the subject of much study. It is generally considered that the means of action is ionic, that is that an electrical charge at a particular site on the catalyst is what activates the polymerization. The polymer appears to remain attached to one site for its entire growing life. The polymerization occurs on the solid surface, that is the monomer is built into the growing chain at its base. The ability of the catalyst to feed monomer units to the chain in precise orienations must stem from the details of the active site and its charges.

Figure 3.6 is a diagram of one suggested structure; in this structure one of the chlorines from the titanium tetrachloride becomes coordinated with the aluminum (dotted lines), while one of the methyls from the aluminum trimethyl coordinates with the titanium atom. This ring type structure undoubtedly results in some unusual electron orbitals which result in the ability to coordinate materials with vinyl structure and cause them to polymerize.

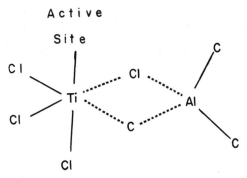

Figure 3.6. A possible configuration for the active site of Ziegler catalyst.

The variety of metal halides and metal alkyls that can produce catalysts of this type is so great that no purpose would be served by compiling a partial list. Metal alkyls were laboratory curiosities when these catalysts were discovered (except for a rather atypical one, tetraethyl lead), and in little over a decade they have become tonnage chemicals. This is especially remarkable when you consider that they ignite spontaneously on contact with air, react explosively with water, and are rather rapidly decomposed by even traces of water. In spite of this, techniques have been worked out that permit them to be made, stored, and used without danger.

Catalysts of this sort are widely used to produce synthetic rubber, as well as plastics, and their ability to control the structure of the rubbers has revolutionized the synthetic rubber industry in the decade after their first introduction.

Phillips Process Catalysts, and others   In the Phillips process the catalyst is chromium oxide supported on silica or silica alumina. The mechanism by which the chromium oxide catalysts work is no better understood than that of the Ziegler type. A recent review of what is known was published in Industrial and Engineering Chemistry by Alfred Clark of the Phillips Petroleum Company. He showed evidence that polymerization occurred by the reaction of an adsorbed monomer molecule with an adjacently adsorbed molecule or growing polymer chain. That is that whatever happens, happens right at the solid surface, but that two different sites are used for each polymer molecule, an adsorption site and a reaction site. He also concluded that the active sites do not all have the same energy, but have a distribution of energy levels.

The nature of the polymer produced depends on the catalyst preparation, as shown in Table 3.6.

TABLE 3.6.   Effect of Activation Temperature on Weight Average Molecular Weight (M_w) of Ethylene Polymer

Catalyst Preparation	Relative M_w
CrO_3 silica, 850°C activation	1
CrO_3 silica, 500°C activation	3.5
Silica calcined at 850°C, dry promoted with CrO_3, 500°C activation	1.2
Silica calcined at 850°C, wet promoted with CrO_3, 500°C activation	2.5

It can be seen that approximately the same results are obtained when the CrO_3 and silica are treated at 850°C together, and when the silica only is treated at 850°C and the combination at 500°C without water contact.

However, if the silica is wetted after the 850°C treatment, and the combination treated at 500°C, then results resemble those of the 500°C activation.

It has been shown that at 500°C or above, water will exist on silica only as hydroxyl ions. It therefore appears that the concentration of hydroxyls is one of the factors that controls molecular weight. These groups may be the adsorption sites of the monomer. Adjacent chromium oxide molecules would then be the polymerization site. The polymer molecule growing on the CrO_3 would then be fed ethylene molecules from the OH groups nearby. This makes the molecules longer if the hydroxyl population is greater.

He also showed that when the weight percent of CrO_3 in the catalyst was reduced from 0.75 to 0.001% the production of polymer per gram of total catalyst decreased, but the production of polymer per gram of chromium oxide increased.

The high activity at extreme dilution indicates that a single CrO_3 molecule is the active site. The decrease of CrO_3 activity as concentration increases indicates that there are only a very few sites that provide the best conditions for polymerization, and other places also allow polymerization but at a lower activity. Figure 3.7 shows a possible active site.

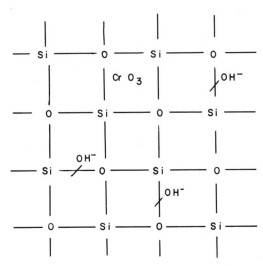

Figure 3.7. A possible configuration for the active catalyst site of Phillips catalyst.

There is one very interesting difference between polyethylene produced by Phillips catalysts and those produced by Ziegler or similar catalysts. The Phillips polymer always has one terminal unsaturation per molecule, while others have less than this, although they may have an equivalent amount of unsaturation elsewhere.

The usual equation for ethylene polymerization such as: $nC_2H_4 \longrightarrow$

$(C_2H_4)_n$ makes no mention of the fact that $(C_2H_4)_n$ is an unsaturated hydrocarbon lacking two hydrogens which would be needed to give a saturated hydrocarbon. The very large size of "n" means that this is a very low degree of unsaturation, but it must be there unless hydrogen is added.

In the case of high pressure polyethylene, the presence of initiator residue or of a hydrogen abstracted from a chain transfer agent or by disproportionation can theoretically saturate the chain. However, some unsaturation is always present.

In the case of solid catalysts, however, there is no means of making a polymer without one unsaturated bond.

The fact that it is always on the end with Phillips resins, and distributed in various locations with Ziegler and other catalysts, shows that there must be a fundamental difference in the mechanism by which the catalysts work.

The presence of this terminal double bond makes the Phillips type resin somewhat more reactive than other resins where the double bond is in a less reactive location. For instance, a polymer molecule can, under some circumstances, enter another growing polymer molecule, producing a long chain branched polymer. When molten, such a branched polymer has the interesting property of being very reluctant to flow at low stresses, yet flows rapidly at high stresses.

It is also necessary to stabilize the Phillips type resins somewhat more to achieve a similar degree of heat stability.

Little has been published about Standard Oil of Indiana catalysts, but their active sites must be similar to those of the Phillips catalyst, except that molybdenum oxide replaces the chromium.

WHAT IS MEANT BY STEREOSPECIFIC

We have mentioned that the various low pressure processes are capable of producing ordered polymers, but we have not heretofore discussed the nature of this order. In order to discuss this we must define some terms and explain some concepts very briefly.

The prefix stereo is used to designate the position of molecules in space. Stereospecific polymerization is therefore polymerization in which the position or orientation of the monomer units of resulting polymer is specific or unchanging.

The term "tactic" is closely related to this. A tactic polymer is a polymer whose monomeric or basic structural units follow one another in a chain with their respective spatial configuration in some particular order.

In the polyolefin plastics two kinds of tacticity dominate. Atactic polymer, which is random or no order, and isotactic polymer, whose building blocks are unsymmetrical, and in which the building blocks are so arranged that, if one passes along the chain from one block to the next, it will be found in the same relative position in space.

You can see that isotactic cannot apply to ethylene polymers, because ethylene is a completely symmetrical molecule. It does, however, apply to all the other olefins, and the significant polyolefin plastics, aside from polyethylene, are all isotactic.

To get any understanding of the meaning of the word isotactic, we have to discuss stereochemistry a little, and explain the meaning of the conventional diagrams which represent the position of molecules in space.

Representing the Carbon Atom

At the beginning of this chapter we explained why it is that the four bonds that a carbon atom makes with other atoms tend to arrange themselves as if they came out of the apices of an equilateral tetrahedron with the carbon atom at the center of the tetrahedron. It is evidently difficult to represent a three dimensional figure on a piece of paper, so we have adopted a conventional representation. In order to visualize this, look at Figure 3.8A and imagine you are looking directly at the transparent face of a tetrahedron, and through it you see the center point and lines running through the apices. Besides the three lines you see, there is one line that goes straight back, and the lines you do see are not in the plane of the paper but are coming out at an angle. For convenience we would like to have at least two of these lines in the plane of the paper, so in Figure 3.8B we have tipped the upper apex of the tetrahedron towards us just enough to get the carbon atom in the center and the bond lines on the right and left into the same plane. In Figure 3.8C we have removed the lines outlining the tetrahedron and left only the bond lines. Bond lines 1 and 3 are in the plane of the paper and make an angle of about 130°

with each other. Bond line 2 projects out in front of the paper at an angle of 65°, and bond line 4 projects behind the paper at the same angle. Figure 3.8 C is the conventional steric representation of a carbon atom.

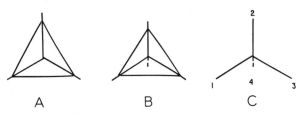

A   B   C

Figure 3.8. Conventional representation of a carbon atom.

Representing a Polymer Chain

Using this as a building block we can then represent a chain of carbon atoms by joining these symbols together. We will use the bonds in the plane of the paper to represent the main chain bonds. This gives us a picture like Figure 3.9. You can see that the symbol is upside down every other time to make the bond angles come out right.

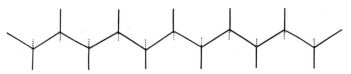

Figure 3.9. Conventional representation of a chain of carbon atoms.

Symmetrical Olefins

If all the bonds not in the plane of the paper are attached to hydrogen atoms, Figure 3.9 represents linear polyethylene. To represent low density or branched polyethylene, we would have to make a very long chain and show one bond on every thirty to fifty carbons attached to a short side branch of two to four carbons.

Unsymmetrical Olefins

The most important use of this sort of diagram, however, is to represent polymers of unsymmetrical olefins. If you refer to Table 3.1 you will see that all the olefins used to produce polyolefin plastics, with the exception of ethylene, are unsymmetrical about the double bond. This means that if we represent their polymers in the form of Figure 3.9, one of the four available bonds from each pair of two carbons will be attached to a hydrocarbon radical (R_2) instead of a hydrogen. If these radicals were distributed randomly between the four bonds, we would have a polymer with no order, an atactic polymer.

In all major commercial polyolefin plastics, however, these radicals are attached to the chain in a perfectly regular order, each monomer unit being oriented just like every other. This is the isotactic form which is represented in Figure 3.10.

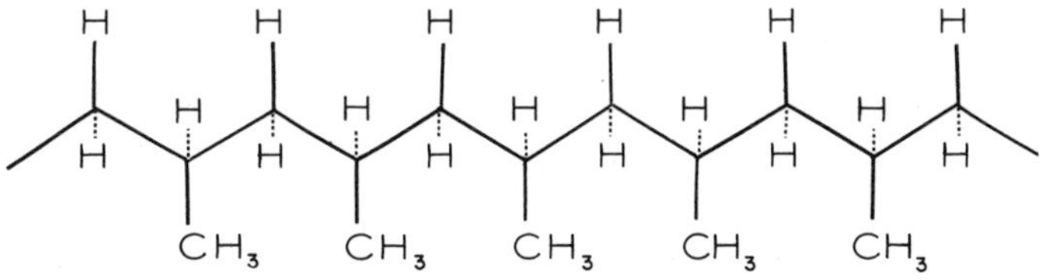

Figure 3.10. Conventional representation of a portion of a polypropylene molecule.

Other Tactic Forms

There are many other ways in which repeat configurations can be built into a polymer. The next simplest is the syndiotactic form, where monomer units alternate with the side hydrocarbons on opposite bonds. Catalysts have been made that produce this form of polymer, and such polymers have interesting characteristics, but none has yet become a major plastic material.

HOW POLYOLEFIN MOLECULES ARE DISPOSED IN SPACE

The method of representing a polymer molecule on a flat piece of paper, as in Figure 3.10, is a very convenient way of showing how the molecule is constructed, but it could be very misleading if we took it to represent the actual way in which the molecule is disposed in space. To understand this, we have to consider that the atoms are not merely dots connected by lines, but that each atom has around it an electrical field which repels every other atom near it. This electrical field is effective over distances longer than the interatomic bond distances, so that all the atoms near each other on the chain influence each other. While the direction and length of each bond is fixed, each atom is entirely free to rotate about the bond joining it to its neighbor. Each atom will therefore rotate in such a way as to balance the repulsions between the atoms.

Since the carbon atoms are much larger and heavier than the hydrogens, they will determine the chain direction.

The Configuration of the Polyethylene Molecule

To start with the simplest case, we will consider a few possible ways in which a polyethylene molecule could extend in space. First let us just look at four carbon atoms as represented in Figure 3.11.

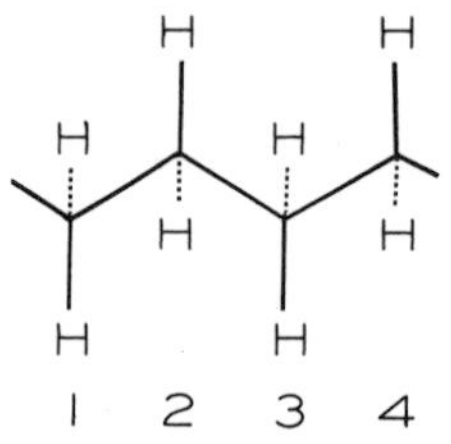

Figure 3.11. Four carbon atoms in normal locations.

This is the same as the plane representation, but now we consider the carbons free to rotate on their bonds.

If the first three atoms stay in place except that the third one rotates on the bond joining it to the second, the fourth carbon atom then leaves the plane of the paper. If we let it rotate 180° it may be represented like in Figure 3.12.

You can see that this has brought carbon 4 nearer to carbons 1 and 2 and subject to greater repulsive force. We could try any other movement of carbon 4, and the same thing will happen. Hence, we see the polyethylene molecule tends to stretch itself out in a planar zigzag, just about as indicated in the conventional diagram. The preferred physical form is therefore a stiff rod. Of course in long lengths this is distorted, and in a mass the presence of other molecules forces it out of shape, but this is its natural form.

It is interesting to consider the differences between linear and branched polyethylene. In branched polyethylene every thirty to fifty carbons will have a side branch on it. Suppose in Figures 3.11 and 3.12 one of the hydrogens on carbon 3 were replaced by a polyethylene branch. Then there would be no difference in the two figures, if you rotated one CH_2 group away from carbon 1 and 2 the other one would get closer, the two positions are equal in repulsion. This means that we have put a swivel point in the molecule at the branch

Figure 3.12. Four carbon atoms with one displaced by rotation about a bond.

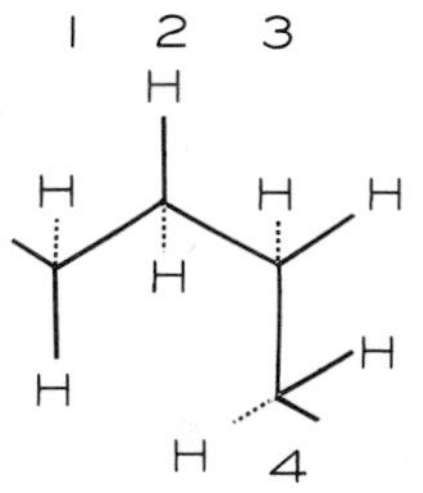

point, making it more flexible, and this corresponds to the difference in physical properties between the two plastics.

The Configuration of Isotactic Molecules

If we think of the molecule shown in Figure 3.10 in the terms we just discussed above, we can readily see that the bulky CH_3 groups are not going to line up in a row when they are not constrained by the paper. What they will do, will be to distribute themselves around the main chain as far away from each other as possible. When they do this the chain will take the form of a spiral, either right or left handed, the exact shape of which depends on the nature of the side group. In the case of polypropylene where the side group is CH_3, the spiral takes the form shown in Figure 3.13. Only the carbon atoms are represented in this drawing.

CRYSTALLIZATION

The polyolefin plastics all have a regular crystal structure, and vary in percent crystallinity from 40-50% in branched polyethylene to over 90% in some of the isotactic types. Some copolymers of ethylene with polar monomers have very little, if any, crystallinity.

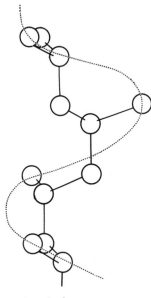

Figure 3.13. Polypropylene molecule disposed in space showing spiral form.

Polyethylene

It has not yet been possible to determine the exact structure of the polyethylene crystal in the solid produced from melt in normal plastics processing. However, very good crystals may be grown from solution and the structure of these has been clearly defined. It is generally assumed that the normal solid contains crystals of the same general nature but small and fragmentary. We have previously noted that the polyethylene molecule is a stiff straight rod. It might be expected that such rods would crystallize by lining up parallel with each other, and this was for years the accepted picture of a polyethylene crystal. Recent studies indicate, however, that it folds back on itself, much like the familiar folding rule used by carpenters, building a flat ribbon crystal with the main chain axis of the molecule at right angles to the length of the crystal. These ribbon crystals stack up with their wide sides together to form flat plates. These crystal plates have been called the telephone switchboard model, because any molecule comes out and then plugs right back in and goes through the plate again. As previously mentioned, these plates form only from solutions, but electron microscope photos of the crystals are quite convincing evidence for the switchboard model. Figure 3.14 represents a slice through a stack of such crystals.

The visible crystalline structure of polyethylene cooled from a

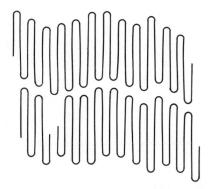

Figure 3.14. Folded polyethylene crystals.

melt is quite different from this. It takes the form of a spherulite, which is a small structure like a pincushion stuck full of very long pins. Each of the pins consists of two or more of the carpenters rule type of crystals joined together. These ribbon crystals radiate from a center or nucleus which started the crystal growing. Hundreds of crystals will radiate from the nucleus, making the visible spherulite. One of the curious things about these structures is their persistence in the molten state. A sample can be melted and held for quite a while well above the melting point, and on cooling will reproduce the same spherulite structure it had before melting, each spherulite in just the same place and the same size.

A branch on a chain will, of course, interfere with the crystallization, and this is why branched polyethylene has a lower density and percent crystallinity than linear. Being less densely packed, branched polyethylene is also not so strong. However, because the branches tend to go between crystals, forming intercrystalline bridges, the branched material is more resistant to creep at low loadings, and also more resistant to stress cracking agents. Much linear polyethylene is copolymerized with a little higher olefin to give a few branches for resistance.

Isotactic Polyolefins

We have noted that the isotactic polyolefins do not form straight rod criystals but rather right and left hand spirals. These materials do not form flat plate crystals. Even when crystallized out of a solution, they take on a spherulite structure. The radiating ribbons in this case being alternating left and right hand spirals interlocked with each other. This interlocking spiral structure holds the chains much more closely together, giving the material higher heat resistance and greater resistance to creep than polyethylene. As the side chain on the isotactic molecule grows larger, the chains cannot come as closely together, so density decreases. The looser packing makes the polymer more flexible, but at the same time the larger side chain makes the spiral deeper, so the interlocking is stronger, and heat resistance and resistance to creep improve.

EFFECT OF COPOLYMERIZATION

Random Copolymers

The effect of copolymerization with higher olefins has been mentioned earlier. This simply interferes with the regularity of the crystal structure, making the polymer less dense, less strong, but more flexible.

When a polar molecule like vinyl acetate or one of the acrylates is used as comonomer, the effect on crystallinity is even more pronounced, and completely amorphous materials may be produced. The presence of the polar group, however, completely changes the nature of the intermolecular forces. In an all olefin polymer the only forces holding molecules together are the weak Van der Waals forces. The polar groups, on the other hand, have relatively strong electrostatic forces associated with them, which produce strong tie spots between molecules. This gives these polar copolymers a structure that is in some ways analogous to rubbers. Of course the electrostatic bond is not as strong as the vulcanized cross-link in a rubber, which is a coordinate bond, but it is much stronger than the intermolecular forces of the hydrocarbon part of the chain. This means that at temperatures below those that loosen the electrostatic bond, these polymers show rubberlike elasticity. That is, they can deform reversibly over fairly large deformations, giving them excellent impact resistance. At the same time the strong polar bonds resist loosening up to temperatures considerably higher than those required to melt the hydrocarbon. This means that the polar copolymers are more flexible at low temperatures, yet more heat resistant than the parent pure olefin, increasing the usable temperature range in both directions.

Ionomers

The ionomers are a very special case of polar copolymers. If a comonomer is used that is capable of forming ionic bonds with metals, acrylic acid is the usual one, then the polymer may be reacted with a metal, the metal then forms what is essentially a salt with the polymer. If the metal is difunctional, such as calcium, the metal may form a bridge between two chains, giving bridge points even stronger and more heat resistant than those formed by the polar groups. This carries the low modulus with heat resistance property combination even further.

Block Copolymers

We get quite different results if, instead of just allowing a comonomer to enter a molecule at random, we build up molecules consisting of fairly long sequences of one monomer unit alternating with fairly long sequences of the other. The way this is done will be explained in Chapter 4. This is called a block copolymer. The first point of difference is that the block copolymer does not lose its crystallinity, if the block sequences are reasonably long they can crystallize just like the homopolymer. However, if they are separated by considerable sequences of noncrystallizable polymer or polymer forming a different type of crystal, then the plastic becomes more flexible. The main commercial use of block copolymer has been to give low temperature toughness to polypropylene, and to improve its room temperature impact strength.

CHEMICAL REACTIONS

The polyolefin plastics are in general quite unreactive chemically, yet the reactions that they do have are quite important both as limitations for some end uses and as a means of modification that extends applications.

Radiation Induced Reactions

Both helpful and harmful effects may be produced in polyolefin plastics by radiation. Pure saturated hydrocarbon materials have little absorption for radiation, however polyolefin plastics all have small amounts of oxygen in them, usually present as carbonyl that is introduced in manufacture or processing, and these groups are very effective radiation absorbers.

Ultraviolet Light   The main harmful effect is chain breakdown from exposure to ultraviolet radiation. Progressive shortening of the polymer chains gradually weakens and embrittles the plastic. Stabilization of the plastic is essential to success in outdoor applications. Two kinds of stabilization are required, the first one is stabilization against oxygen attack to reduce the number of absorptive groups in the molecule. This will be discussed later. The second one is stabilization by shielding against ultraviolet light. The most effective material for this purpose is carbon black. Two percent or more of well dispersed fine particle size carbon black will almost completely shield any polyolefin against deterioration by the ultraviolet in sunlight. In case a colorless plastic is needed, the problem is not so simple. A considerable variety of ultraviolet absorbers is known, and some of them give considerable protection to polyolefins. They do not, however, give anything like the protection given by carbon black, and they are fairly expensive.

The first ultraviolet stabilizers used in polyolefin plastics were esters of salicylic acid. These must be used in fairly high concentrations to be effective and have some undesirable side reactions. They have been largely replaced by o-hydroxybenzophenones, substituted benzotriazoles, and substituted acrylonitriles which are effective in lower concentrations. Recently some phenolic chelates of nickel have been introduced, which are interesting in that they do not themselves absorb ultraviolet radiation but still protect the plastic. They are not widely applicable because they color the polymer somewhat.

Table 3.7 shows the chemical formulas of some representative ultraviolet absorbers.

It should be mentioned that except for thin films the deterioration

TABLE 3.7. Light Stabilizers for Polyolefins

Name	Formula
2-(2'-Hydroxyphenyl) benzotriazoles	
o-Hydroxybenzophenones	
Substituted acrylonitriles	
Salicylates	

due to ultraviolet radiation tends to be self-limiting, because the deteriorated polymer develops large numbers of carbonyl groups which are excellent ultraviolet absorbers and so shield the main body of plastic from the rays.

Gamma Radiation   The main useful effect produced by radiation is polyethylene cross-linking by gamma radiation. Gamma radiation produced by an electron gun, or by nuclear means can be used to cross-link polyethylene. By hydrogen abstraction the radiation produces reactive sites on the molecule and causes it to join up with an adjacent molecule as shown in Figure 3.15.

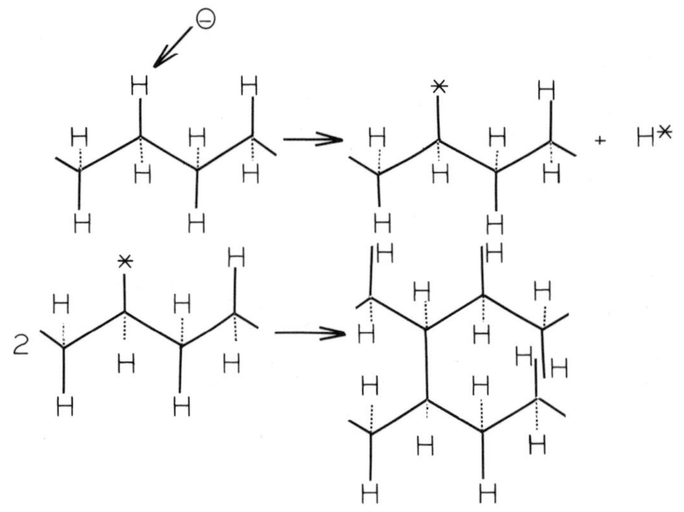

Figure 3.15. The polyethylene cross-linking reaction.

Since the susceptibility of hydrogens to abstraction depends on the carbon to which it is attached and varies as follows: Tertiary > Secondary > Primary, this process works most readily with branched polyethylene, where there is a supply of tertiary carbons at the branch points.

It might be supposed that the unsymmetrical polyolefins, which have half their carbons tertiary would be particularly useful in this reaction. The fact is that the high concentration of tertiary carbon atoms makes these materials much more inclined to chain rupture when irradiated, and useful cross-linking is achieved only with difficulty.

The usefulness of the cross-linking is that it forms the molecules into a network tied together with carbon–carbon bonds. Such a structure is more heat resistant; in fact it is no longer thermoplastic, so irradiation must be done on final products. The use of this technique in making shrink film will be discussed in Chapter 5. This cross-linked material is also stronger and less susceptible to certain agents that normally attack polyethylene.

Chemical Cross-linking

Cross-linking may also be induced in polyethylene by the use of peroxides or other free radical sources. The reaction is the same as that shown for radiation induced cross-linking, but the free radical source is an unstable chemical rather than a gamma ray.

In this process the peroxide is mixed into the molten polymer, which is then pelletized. The pelletized compound is then reextruded into its final form and cross-linked by exposure to a higher temperature in its final form. This evidently presents some serious problems, the first of which is supporting the plastic and maintaining its shape at the higher temperature before cross-linking sets in. This problem has so far limited the use of chemical cross-linking almost entirely to electrical wire insulation, where the insulation can be supported by the wire during this critical period.

The other major problem is that the decomposition range of the free radical source is extremely critical. It must be stable enough to withstand polymer melt temperatures during compounding and extrusion, without forming any substantial numbers of cross-links which would prevent smooth extrusion. It must also decompose at a temperature low enough so that the coating does not melt and run off before the reaction is completed, and also the reaction must be fast enough to allow cross-linking at high extrusion speeds. These limitations have so far been met successfully only by cumene peroxide and a few proprietary materials. Cumene peroxide has a side reaction which produces acetophenone which has a strong odor and lacrimatory properties. This means that most cross-linked polyethylene has a bad odor.

Reactions with Oxygen

Like any hydrocarbon, the polyolefin plastics burn. However, they also react with oxygen at a slower rate at temperatures well below their ignition temperatures. In fact, at normal processing temperatures polyolefin plastic melts absorb oxygen quite rapidly. The oxygen absorbed first produces carbonyl and ester groups along the chain, and then removes hydrogen in the form of water. This process results in loss of physical properties due to chain breaking, discoloration due to an accumulation of double bonds, and in the case of polyethylene some cross-linking.

Antioxidants   This means that the polyolefin must be protected from this reaction by an antioxidant. A wide variety of antioxidants is used for different polyolefins, and for different end uses. For formulations that are used in contact with food, the BHT and BHA which are used to stabilize cooking oils are very common. A partial list is shown in Table 3.8.

TABLE 3.8.   Antioxidants for Polyolefins

2,2-Methylenebis(4,6-methyl-*tert*-butylphenol)
2,6-Di-tert-butyl-*para*-cresol (BHT)
Aryl phosphites
Aryl-alkyl phosphites
Dilauryl thiodipropionate (DLTDP)
Distearyl thiodroprionate (DSTDP)

How Antioxidants Work   To understand what the antioxidant does, we must first understand how oxygen attacks the polyolefin. At processing temperatures the polymer itself, or impurities such as catalyst residues or catalyst decomposition products, form a few free radicals. The free radicals react with oxygen to form peroxy radicals.

$$R^* + O_2 \longrightarrow ROO^*$$

These abstract a hydrogen from a polymer and form a hydroperoxide, and another polymer free radical.

$$ROO^* + R_1H \longrightarrow ROOH + R_1{}^*$$

The hydroperoxides finally decompose, breaking the polymer chain and forming a new free radical.

Antioxidants can prevent this reaction either by tying up the peroxy radicals so that they cannot propagate the reaction, or by decomposing the hydroperoxides so that additional radicals are not formed. The first group are called free radical scavengers or inhibitors and are usually phenols or amines. The second group are called peroxide decomposers and are generally sulfur compounds or metal complexes. It is very common to use one material from each group in combination, since such combinations are often more effective than either alone.

Other Chemical Reactions

Chlorination   Polyolefins can be chlorinated directly with gaseous chlorine either in solution or in finely divided form. The presence of ultraviolet light or other activator is necessary to make the reaction go at practical rates. Commercially, chlorinated polyethylene is available over a wide range of chlorine contents, forming a very useful line of plastics ranging from soft rubber materials to hard stiff ones. Chlorination makes polyethylene noninflammable, and this opens up new applications.

Chlor-sulfonation   The product from the reaction of polyethylene with chlorine and sulfur dioxide was the first commercial chemical derivative of polyethylene. It has maintained a considerable market for many years, but the product goes into elastomeric rather than strictly plastics uses.

ADDITIVES USED IN POLYOLEFINS

A polyolefin plastic compound consists of a resin, and a series of minor ingredients that give the compound special and use properties. Some of these have already been mentioned under ultraviolet light screening and antioxidants. There are also some others used, whose function is physical rather than chemical. However, since much of this chapter concerns the ingredients that go into a polyolefin compound, it seems more appropriate to mention them here than elsewhere.

Slip Additives

In many polyolefin applications, particularly film and coatings, but to a lesser extent in some injection molded and extruded parts, it is desirable to have the surface coefficient of friction lower than the one that would result from the use of unmodified resin. It is, of course, possible to coat the finished article with a dust or spray for this purpose, but here we are discussing only those materials that are added to the plastic compound before final processing. Slip additives belong to the general class of surface active agents in that they have a polar and nonpolar end. The polar end causes them to be rejected from the plastic mass, while the nonpolar end remains firmly attached. This means that, although they start mixed into the plastic mass they soon "bloom" to the surface and form a surface layer. In addition to this, the surface layer so formed has to have a low coefficient of friction. There are quite a few materials that will do this, and for such purposes as keeping molded parts from sticking when stacked, or making a polyethylene insulated wire slip in a conduit, there is a wide choice of materials.

Slip additive technology has been particularly highly developed in the polyolefin film business, where a slip additive has stringent limitations. It must not spoil the optical properties of the film, must not interfere with printing or heat sealing, and must be odorless, colorless, and nontoxic.

These requirements, in conjunction with acceptance by the Food and Drug Administration, have limited polyolefin slip additives to a small group of fatty acid amides, especially oleamide, stearamide, and erucamide.

The materials used are commercial products manufactured from natural oils and fats, so they are by no means pure chemical compounds. This means that the products sold by the same name by different manufacturers may differ not merely in matters of color and odor but also in chemical composition, and behave quite differently in use. A manufacturer will generally obtain his raw materials from the same source and by blending will try to maintain a uniform product, but the user has to be very careful to assure uniformity.

Antiblock Additives

These have the function of keeping two polyolefin surfaces from sticking together, without, however, making the surface slippery. In many cases a slip additive performs this function quite adequately, but, especially in the case of films, slip additives will not suffice. The reason for this is that the polyolefin films are often very smooth and glossy, so that they conform so closely when pressed together as to exclude air from between them. A slip additive film may make this problem worse rather than better. What is needed is something to produce a slight roughness to allow the air to pass in. The antiblock additives generally used in film are some very fine grades of diatomaceus earth. If the particle size is too small, it will not produce enough surface roughness to prevent blocking. If it is too coarse the appearance of the film will be spoiled, so very careful choice is necessary.

The antiblock function can, of course, also be taken care of by purely mechanical means, such as embossing the surface. This is the method generally used for polyolefin coatings.

Antistatic Additives

Polyolefin plastic objects have a great tendency to accumulate a static charge which attracts dust, causes clinging of film to conversion equipment, and is otherwise detrimental. This problem can be handled by surface treatments but these are very temporary, and the best results are obtained by agents incorporated into the compound. Like slip additive, these materials must have a limited compatability with the resin which will cause them to form an adherent film on the surface. This film must be electrically conductive to dissipate static electricity.

The materials being used are ethoxylated aliphatic amines and amides, ethylene oxide adducts of aliphatic hydrocarbons, phosphate esters, quarternary ammonium salts, and glycol esters. There is no ideal material for all purposes, each has its special use.

Blowing Agents

Polyolefin foams may be produced by direct use of gas or volatile liquids. Here we are concerned with solid materials incorporated at the time of manufacture, which will cause a polyolefin plastic compound to foam when processed. The most satisfactory materials for this purpose are certain organic compounds that liberate gases when heated. Typical examples are shown in Table 3.9.

There are also proprietary materials available whose exact composition is not publicized.

TABLE 3.9. Foaming Agents Used in Polyolefin Plastics

Compound	Foaming Temperature °C
Azobisformamide (azodicarbonamide)	160-200
N,N'-Dinitrosopentamethylenetetramine	130-190
4,4'-Oxybis(benzenesulfonylhydrazide)	120-140

FOUR

the manufacture of polyolefin plastics

OLEFIN PRODUCTION

The development of any polyolefin plastic must necessarily be preceded by the development of an adequate supply of the olefin monomer, at a price which will make the polymer attractive. In this sense the polyolefin plastic is just one end result of the development of the petrochemical industry.

The ethylene used in Britain for the original production of polyethylene was made from coal by the roundabout and rather expensive method of making calcium carbide from coal and limestone, and reacting the calcium carbide with water to produce acetylene, and then hydrogenating acetylene to get ethylene.

At present most ethylene is produced from petroleum or from natural gas. The development of this industry has reached the state where any refinery stream from light gas to heavy naptha can be used as feedstock for an ethylene plant. Which feedstock is used depends on the value of the stream at the particular location. Ethylene can even be made directly from crude oil. This makes it possible to build an ethylene plant at a location away from an oil refinery. Ethylene plants have increased in size and efficiency, making them a very attractive investment at the present time. This has naturally attracted new producers into the field and encouraged the old ones to expand, resulting in an adequate supply of ethylene at a cost which will probably decrease for some time even in the face of general cost increases. This will improve the competitive position of polyolefins in comparison with that of products not based on ethylene. Most ethylene plants produce some propylene as a by-product, and many can be operated in such a way as to control the ratios of the two products.

Ethylene and propylene are produced from feedstocks consisting of a wide variety of hydrocarbons, saturated and unsaturated. This feedstock is thermally cracked, usually with the assistance of catalysts, to give a mixture of the desired olefins and both lighter and heavier materials. These are separated by distillation to produce pure olefins, while the unwanted products may be recycled or used for other purposes, depending on the most economic path.

The higher olefins are not yet readily available commodities, and the decision to make a polymer from them generally depends upon developing a monomer source. Specialists in this field are developing, and processes are available for making almost any olefin. However, in most cases the higher olefin will be considerably more expensive than ethylene or propylene, so the corresponding polymer must have some special properties to justify the added cost.

HIGH PRESSURE POLYETHYLENE

The high pressure process, originally developed by ICI *, is still the way in which the largest tonnage of polyolefins is made. This process is capable of making polyethylene ranging from hard, high density material through soft, rubbery copolymers. For economic reasons, however, its use is generally limited to polyethylenes in the low and middle density ranges, and to copolymers with polar comonomers such as vinyl acetate or the acrylic esters.

The process is carried out at pressures of from 15,000-50,000 psi and at temperatures from 200-500°F. Under these conditions ethylene is above its critical temperature, so it remains in the gaseous state, however it is compressed to a density that makes it behave like lubricating oil.

* Imperial Chemical Industries.

Types of Equipment

The process is carried out in two general types of equipment, long tubes and stirred autoclaves. The tubes are generally between $\frac{3}{4}$ inch and $1\frac{1}{2}$ inches in diameter, and several hundred feet long. The autoclaves differ greatly in design among manufacturers, ranging from cylinders about the same length and diameter to cylinders 12 or 15 times as long as their diameter. The stirrer motors are sometimes included inside the pressure shell to avoid the problems associated with maintaining a packing on a moveable shaft at these pressures. Details of reactor geometry influence the properties of the resin produced.

The largest producers of high pressure polyethylene use both tubular reactors and stirred autoclaves, because certain grades of polyethylene are more readily made on one or the other. However, some manufacturers make a complete line of resins using only one kind of reactor.

The polymerization of ethylene in a high pressure reactor is extremely rapid, producing a complete polymer molecule in a fraction of a second. This means that a small reactor has a very large output. Ethylene polymerization is highly exothermic, so the production of polymer is limited to the amount of heat that can be handled. Because of the high rate of reaction, it is not usually possible to remove any significant proportion of the heat by heat transfer to the walls of the reactor. This means that only as much polymer can be made at a pass as will heat up the reacting mass to the maximum temperature that can be tolerated in the production of the particular resin being made. This generally limits conversion to 10-15% of the gas by weight at a pass. At one time a process was operated which used water as a heat control medium in the reactor, but the problems associated with separation of water and polymer make this unattractive. Tubular reactors, because of their greater ratio of surface area to volume, can transfer a larger proportion of the heat of reaction than an autoclave reactor and can therefore get more conversion per pass.

After passing through the reactor, the gas is separated from the polymer, cooled, compressed, and recycled through the reactor, while the polymer is extruded through a die, pelletized, and cooled. Figure 4.1 shows a generalized diagram of this process.

The reactions that go on in this process have been described in Chapter 3. Here we are concerned with how they are carried out in practice.

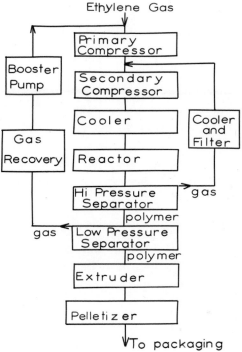

Figure 4.1. A simplified flow sheet of the high-pressure polyethylene process.

Initiator Handling

The reaction initiator, generally a peroxide, is highly inflammable, temperature sensitive, and in some cases can be detonated by shock. Refrigerated storage is commonly required, and it is general practice to use the initiator in relatively dilute solution in an inert solvent to make it more stable. This also facilitates the accurate metering of the relatively small amounts used and permits ready disperson in the reaction mix.

Initiator solution is pumped directly into the reactor in the exact amounts needed to maintain the reaction at the conditions desired.

Initiator injection points vary with the reactor design. In the case of tubular reactors or long autoclaves there may be several injection points throughout the length of the reactor. The location of injection points serves to control molecular weight distribution in the resulting polymer.

Requirements for a Reactor

The highly exothermic propagation reaction is very rapid, and this requires excellent mixing in an autoclave or high gas velocity in a tube, to prevent the formation of hot spots from excessive initiator concentrations. Hot spots can produce an explosive reaction known as a "decomp", which results in a very sudden rise in pressure and temperature, which is capable of destroying the reactor unless properly vented. Reactors are generally built with one or more large openings to a vent stack, which are closed by rupture discs which release the contents of the reactor out the vent in case excessive pressures are built up. Because of the extremely rapid buildup of pressure in a "decomp", these have to be very quick acting to be effective, so specially designed disks must be used.

Reactor Control

Chain transfer agents are also added to the reactor to control polymer properties. The primary control of polymer chain length is reactor temperature and pressure. Temperature and pressure, however, also influence other properties, such as chain branching. The chain transfer agent gives control of chain length independent of pressure and temperature, and so makes possible combinations of properties not possible without it.

Chain transfer agents are generally added to the reaction gas prior to the final compressor but may also be injected directly into the reactor.

Termination occurs by coupling or disproportionation of free radicals in the reactor and is controlled by reactor temperature; the higher the temperature the more frequent the terminations, and therefore the shorter the molecules.

Separation

After leaving the reactor the mixture of polymer and unreacted ethylene goes to a separator, where the pressure is dropped to something between 1500 and 3000 pounds. The gas expands greatly and separates from the polymer readily. The gas is then filtered and returned to the suction of the secondary compressor.

The polymer, with some dissolved gas, goes to a low pressure separator, at essentially atmospheric pressure, where the remainder of the gas is released. This gas may be purified, recompressed, and returned to the system, or it may leave the process for some other use.

The polymer is removed from the bottom of the separator by a screw extruder and pelletized in any one of the ways that will be described later.

Additives may be put into the polymer by injection into the final separator, or into the screw extruder, or by subsequent blending or compounding operations.

Advantages and Limitations

The wide range of temperatures and pressures over which this process can be operated, the wide differences in reactor design possible, and the possibilities inherent to the use of different initiators, chain transfer agents, and other reaction modifiers, make it possible to produce a very wide variety of different polymers by this process. When the possibilities of copolymerization are added to this, it can be seen that this is an extremely versatile process.

Despite the costs inherent in pumping gas up to the extremely high pressures used in this process, the process is basically simple and low in cost. This combination makes it quite probable that the largest production of polyethylene will continue to be by the high pressure process for a long time to come. This process is not, however, well adapted to the production of other polyolefins, which must be made by one of the low pressure processes.

Safety Considerations in the High Pressure Process

Since its inception the high pressure process for making polyethylene has been plagued by disasterous explosions. This is not, as often assumed, due to the rupture of the high pressure reactors. Some of the very first explosions at ICI were due to this cause, but reactor design and venting have rendered pressure surges in the reactors harmless.

The main present danger lies in the fact that at pressures of 15,000 psi or over, a very large amount of gas can escape from a very small leak in a short time. Ethylene gas produces explosive mixtures with air over a very wide concentration range. The usual hazard is that an unnoticed gas leak accumulates a large amount of an explosive mixture of ethylene and air around the plant and that this is then accidentally ignited.

The high pressure polyethylene manufacturers have cooperated very closely to develop safety standards for these plants. These include all welded piping, except where it is absolutely necessary to be able to break a line, and special flanges there; high volume forced ventilation of all areas in which a gas leak could develop; the use of automatic alarms to detect gas in all danger areas, and stringent precautions to eliminate all possible sources of ignition in the danger areas.

In addition to this, personnel is often protected by the use of remote control of the high pressure equipment, and the use of reinforced concrete block house type control rooms.

While this process must always remain an inherently hazardous one, the lessons learned from the previous accidents have been carefully acted upon, and in the future it should be no more hazardous than other large scale chemical processes using highly inflammable materials.

LOW PRESSURE PROCESSES

While there are a great many differences in detail between the low pressure processes for making the various polyolefins, the similarities are so great that the purposes of this book will be best served by handling them all together. There are also several different processes for each polyolefin based on different catalyst systems, but all have strong basic similarities, so will be handled together, and the differences noted as necessary. A general flow sheet for a low pressure process is shown in Figure 4.2.

In the low pressure processes for olefin polymerization the reaction takes place at active locations on the surface of a solid catalyst. The solid catalyst may be silica, or silica alumina impregnated with a small amount of metal oxide. In the Phillips process the metal oxide is chromium oxide, in the Standard Oil of Indiana it is molybdenum oxide. In both of these processes other metals or nonmetals may be used in one form or another to promote or modify the action of the catalyst in some way. Also the catalyst must undergo a pretreatment or "activation" process before it will work. The exact details of this activation process are often of more importance than the chemical composition of the catalyst, as has been discussed in Chapter 3. In the Ziegler or Ziegler–Natta process the catalyst is a complex formed by the reaction of an aluminum alkyl with a group IV metal halide, a typical example being aluminum tri-isobutyl and titanium tetrachloride. In these catalysts too, the exact method of preparation, crystal form, etc., are very important. In all of these processes the catalyst production technology is the most important feature of the process. The catalyst preparation and activation techniques determine not simply the activity or efficiency of the catalyst, but the properties of the resin produced as well. Phillips and Standard Oil catalysts must be prepared and activated before contacting the reacting mix. Ziegler catalysts can be made by putting the separate components into the reactor, but are usually made separately.

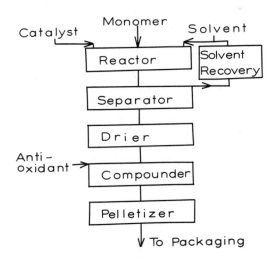

Figure 4.2. A simplified flow sheet of the low-pressure process for polymerizing olefins.

Catalyst Handling

Catalyst handling is also extremely critical. The metal oxide catalysts are not dangerous to handle, but once they are activated they
must be protected from oxygen and from the slightest trace of moisture or other catalyst poisons which will make them completely useless on contact. The Ziegler catalysts are, in addition to being extremely sensitive to poisons, so highly reactive that they will burst
into flame on exposure to air. A whole new technology of absolute
dessication and protection from the atmosphere has been developed
to handle these materials.

The use of these catalysts also requires very stringent standards
of olefin purity, for all the monomers used. Traces of moisture un-
detectable by any ordinary means will destroy the catalyst. Many
other impurities in the olefin that would cause no trouble at all
in free radical polymerization will absolutely prevent low pressure polymerization, or drastically reduce catalyst efficiency.

Advantages of This Process

In view of these difficulties, what makes this process desirable?

There are many factors. The main factor is that this process can
make resins with properties almost unattainable by free radical polymerization. In ethylene polymerization a practically branch-free
polymer can be made with higher density, stiffness, and strength.
Such polymers can also be made by the high pressure process, but
only at prohibitive cost. With the higher olefins the low pressure
process becomes the only one that can make polymers suitable for
plastics applications. Free radical polymers of these materials are
soft rubbery materials. The reason for this difference was explained
in Chapter 3, but briefly it is because the solid catalyst is able to coordinate the olefin in such a way as to control its position as it enters
the polymer chain.

Another important advantage of the low pressure process is that
it operates at low pressure. This saves the high pumping costs inherent to the high pressure process, and makes it possible to use
reactors of light and comparatively inexpensive construction.

Another advantage is that the solid catalysts are extremely efficient. Unlike the free radical initiators they are not consumed in the reaction, so they can go on producing polymer indefinitely until they are poisoned by some impurity. Productivities in the 5,000-6,000 pounds per pound range can be obtained on a regular production basis. This means that catalyst costs are extremely low in this process compared to free radical initiator costs, where a pound of initiator may make only a few hundred pounds of polymer. The oxide type catalysts are also quite inexpensive per pound compared to organic peroxides. The Ziegler type of catalyst is more expensive, but considering productivity is no more so than free radical initiators.

A further advantage of the low pressure process is that the rate of reaction is slow enough so that the heat of reaction can be removed from the reactor by conduction, making it possible to get substantially complete conversion of olefin to polymer at one pass, obviating the recycling required in the high pressure process, and the attendant need for a gas purification system.

The slow reaction rate has another advantage. A single polymer molecule will be growing for periods of an hour or more. This makes it very convenient to make a special kind of copolymer by this process. The high pressure process forms a complete molecule in a fraction of a second. The only way a copolymer can be made in this process is to mix the two monomers together in the reactor, and the two monomers will enter the chain just by chance in any order. This is called a random copolymer. Most low pressure copolymers are made in the same way, producing random copolymers. However, improved properties are possible in some cases by making a block copolymer. To make such a copolymer the solid catalyst is exposed alternately to one monomer and then to the other. The slow rate of growth of the molecule in the low pressure process makes it quite easy to alternate monomers a number of times in the same molecule. This polymer will then consist of a chain segment formed entirely from one monomer, followed by a chain segment formed entirely from the other monomer and so on. Such a copolymer will have different properties from a random copolymer.

Alternative Methods of Operation

The low pressure process is usually carried out in the presence of an inert hydrocarbon solvent, although some solid catalysts can be used in pure gas, without solvent. The solvent acts as a heat control and transfer medium, a means of obtaining good dispersion of the catalyst, and a carrier for the polymer in the process.

Low pressure polymerization may be carried out under two very different sets of conditions, in one of which the polymer dissolves in the solvent, and in the other of which the polymer is insoluble in the solvent and builds up around the catalyst particles in the form of a porous granule.

Selection of solvent is one of the critical determinants of how the process will operate, the more active solvents of course tending toward solution. Temperature and type of polymer are also important, high temperatures and soluble types of polymer giving solution type polymerization.

All of the catalyst systems may be used in both solution and particle form polymerization. Although traditionally there has been preference for one or the other with a particular catalyst system, the pressure to broaden the product line has resulted in the use of both with all of the catalyst systems.

Catalyst Removal

Catalyst removal is one of the most difficult and expensive steps in low pressure olefin polymer production.

In the case of the highly reactive Ziegler catalysts the activity has to be destroyed before removal. The alkali metal promoted Standard of Indiana catalysts also need pretreatment. In either case, simple washing with water or alcohol will render the catalyst inactive. Phillips type catalysts are not dangerously reactive in air, so can be removed without pretreatment. In the case of solution form polymer, the catalyst residue can be removed simply by filtration or centrifuging. In the case of particle form polymer, the polymer must first be dissolved in an active solvent.

The development of the modern superactive catalysts has made it possible in many cases to eliminate the catalyst removal step, because the small amount of catalyst required can be left in the polymer without affecting its value. This reduces the cost of the polymer considerably. Especially in the case of particle form polymerization, avoiding catalyst removal greatly reduces the cost of solvent recovery. A filterable linear polyethylene solution will not contain more than five or six percent polymer. This means that twenty pounds of solvent have to be recovered for each pound of resin produced. A particle form slurry can be handled at a solids content of 30-50%, thus reducing solvent requirements to one tenth or less.

The polymer produced either by precipitation from solution or from drying a slurry consists of very fine particles that are not convenient to use in conventional plastics processing equipment. Recent developments, which will be discussed in Chapter 7, are making it possible to use this resin "fluff" directly, but at present it is necessary to put it into pellet or granule form.

Finishing Operations

For this purpose the dried resin fluff must be put through some sort of machine which will melt it and force the melt through a die, which forms a pellet of appropriate size.

A wide variety of machines is used for this purpose. There are two general sorts of machines used: screw extruders, and intensive mixers. The screw extruders again fall into two classes: single screw machines, and double screw machines. Since the single screw extruder will be discussed in detail under processing we will not consider it any further here. The double screw extruder, and the intensive mixer, however, are used mainly in resin production, and, consequently, belong in this chapter.

Intensive Mixers   The original intensive mixer was the Banbury * mixer. This machine consists of a very heavy jacketed housing containing two lobed rotating shafts. The lobe on the shaft is of such a size that it has only a very narrow clearance from the housing, and it is set at an angle to the line of the shaft. Polymer is put into this machine and pressed strongly into the space between the rotors and housing by means of a hydraulic ram. The rapidly turning rotors then press it against the housing, and also transfer it back and forth

* Trademark: The Farrel Corporation.

between the rotors creating a great deal of frictional heat which rapidly melts the polymer and forms it into a dough-like mass. The great power of these machines results in a complete fusion of a charge in a few minutes. The mass is then dropped out of the machine by opening a door in the bottom, and fed into a hot melt extruder. This machine has had considerable development and refinement recently. For plastics processing the double lobed rotors have been replaced by four lobed rotors which reduce the time required for melting. Other manufacturers have come into the field with machines of similar but slightly different design. The intensive mixer has also been modified for continuous rather than batch operation. In this form there are conveyor screws at the end of the rotor which carry the unmelted resin into the mixing space between the rotors at one end, and then remove molten resin from the mixing space at the other and force it out through an orifice. These machines do not produce enough pressure on the molten polymer to force it through a small opening pellet die, so the production of the continuous mixer is fed to a hot melt extruder for pelletizing. The operation of the extruder, however, is considerably simplified by having a continuous stream of feed, rather than having to contend with a succession of batch loads.

Double Screw Extruder   Double screw extruders are available in considerable variety. Basically they consist of two helical screws rotating in a long chamber with a cross section approximating a figure eight. The screws may rotate in the same direction, or in opposite directions, and they may intermesh in varying degrees. This means that the lands of one screw may penetrate into the grooves of the other screw either fully or partially. The helical flights may also be interrupted and modified in various ways. For instance, sections of the helix may be replaced by lobed disks which interact with the walls of the chamber and with similar disks on the other screw, in much the same way as the rotors of an intensive mixer. The screws may be the same length, or one may be considerably longer than the other. In the latter case we have essentially a double screw extruder feeding into a single screw extruder, except that both are part of the same machine. The types most commonly used in pelletizing polyolefin plastics are counterrotating, partially penetrating, unequal length screws, and screws made up of combinations of spiral and lobed segments, although other types are undoubtedly used to some extent.

Other Finishing Machines Another pelletizing machine used to some extent does not fall into either of these classes. This is the Ko-Kneader *, which consists of a screw with multiple interrupted spiral flights operating in a barrel which is studded with heavy pins. In operation this screw has a combination of rotary and reciprocating motion, whereby the pins pass between the flights and through the interrupted areas in the flights, while the polymer is forwarded by the rotation of the screw.

There is no general agreement about which machine is best, and, in all probability, each has some special applications for which it has an advantage.

FINISHING STEPS COMMON TO BOTH PROCESSES

Pelletizing

The machines described produce a plastic mass under sufficient pressure to force it through a die. The way in which this is converted into a pellet may vary a good deal. Very generally there are three pelletizing methods.

Cube Cut Strip The polymer may be forced through a slit die, cooled until solid, and the resulting strip fed into a rotary cutter, which chops the strip into nearly cubical pellets.

Cut Strand In this method a die with a large number of small holes is used. These holes may be round, square, or even triangular. The polymer is extruded through the die, the strands are cooled and chopped into short pieces by a rotary blade cutter. This makes short cylinders or prisms.

Die Face Cut In this method the same general type of die is used as in the previous method, but instead of drawing a strand from the die, the hot extrudate is cut off by a rapidly moving blade at the die face. This is generally done under water; it is called underwater pelletizing. It is also possible to do the same thing by extruding into air and arranging it so that the cutter throws the pellet into water as

---

* Trademark: Baker Perkins Corporation.

soon as it is cut, to prevent hot pellets sticking together. This method produces pellets of the general shape of a distorted sphere. It is the most common method of pelletizing polyolefin plastics. This form of pellet is especially desirable in case the plastic is being transferred by air conveyor because the spherical shape produces less fines during transfer. The only disadvantage of this type pellet is that in certain dry coloring operations it is more difficult to get good distribution of color, because of the smaller surface area and the generally smoother surface.

Blending and Compounding

Polyolefin resins are susceptible to thermal degradation, so they must have a heat stabilizer, generally called an antioxidant, incorporated into them. Depending on the end use, it may also be necessary to add other materials. These materials are described in Chapter 3; here we are only concerned with how they are put in. It is also often desirable to mix two kinds of resin to get properties impossible to attain in a directly reacted material, or to take advantage of the economics of a process that does not conveniently make a resin of the desired properties.

Dry Blending   The simplest and least expensive method of mixing materials into the resin is by a dry blender. Low pressure process fluff or pellets may be used as starting material. The additive must be in a form that will not segregate from the resin when mixed with it and must not tend to coat on the walls of the mixer. Liquid additives are usually sprayed into the mixing resin in a fine spray. Powdered additives such as pigments or dyes may be added directly to the mixer; however, it is commonly desirable to precoat the resin with a small amount of oil or similar liquid to improve adhesion of the pigment, especially in the case of pellets.

In the case of additives that are required in very small amounts, it is often impossible to get a good enough distribution of material by direct addition, and even in cases where the amounts are larger, better mixtures can be obtained by masterbatch methods. In a masterbatch the additive is first hot melt blended into a portion of the base resin, or a compatible resin of slightly different properties, at a higher concentration than that needed in the final product. This can be done in many of the kinds of equipment described under finishing operations. Intensive mixers are very commonly used. When blending with pellets it is then possible to make the masterbatch with the same pellet size and shape as the base resin, so that when they are mixed together there is no tendency to segregate.

Equipment Used in Dry Blending   The most generally used equipment is the double cone blender. This is a vessel with two conical ends joined by a short cylindrical section. Trunnions are fitted to the center section and mounted on bearings so that the entire vessel can be rotated end over end. These can be made in large sizes, so that if desired, a 100,000 pound batch can be mixed at one time. The blender is filled about half full of the materials to be blended and rotated until they are well mixed.

The twin shell blender is also used a good deal. It consists of two cylinders that intersect in the form of a vee. It is also mounted on trunnions in such a way as to rotate the vee end over end. If continuous rather than batch blending is desired, a succession of vee's can be jointed together and the entire assembly rotated, with components being fed continuously into one end and mix removed continuously at the other.

For small batches a cylindrical vessel, such as a 50 gallon drum may be mounted so that it is at an angle to a shaft and rotated.

Rotary blenders consisting of a cylinder fitted with baffles, and rotated on the axis of the cylinder are also used. The baffles then carry a portion of the contents up as they rotate, and dump it down into the remainder when they near the top of the rotation, producing a mixing action. This is generally similar to the action of a cement mixer.

A special sort of dry blender is called an intensive dry mixer. This must be distinguished from the intensive melt mixer, such as the Banbury * which was described earlier. In the intensive dry mixer there are very rapidly rotating blades which strike the particles of the mix and impinge them violently against the walls of the mixer. Due to the tough nature of polyolefin plastics, this produces little reduction in particle size but serves to imbed small additive particles into the pellets so that they are firmly bound and will not separate in later handling.

* Registered trademark: Farrel Corporation.

Dry blends are often quite satisfactory for use in plastics processing equipment, but in some cases it is necessary to produce a more uniform mixture or to modify the properties of the compound by more drastic mixing.

Hot Melt Mixing

The best possible plastic blends are made by means of hot melt mixers. The intensive hot melt mixer is the most widely used for this purpose. In case of the batch type, weighed amounts of resin or resins and additives are added to each batch and fluxed. In the continuous ones, belt, screw, or vibratory feeders are used to meter the correct proportions of materials into one end, and mixture is discharged at the other. These hot melt mixtures must then be pelletized.

Single screw or multiple screw extruders may also be used. For compounding service these are generally designed so as to give a more intensive mixing action than similar machines used only for pelletizing.

Transferring Pellets or Resin Fluff

Raw resin and finished product pellets are ordinarily moved from place to place by air conveyors. These consist of relatively large diameter pipes designed with very gradual turns, through which a high velocity air stream is blown. The plastic pellets or fluff are dropped into this air stream, either in a continuous flow or in small portions by means of a star feeder. They are then swept through the pipe by the air stream to the destination. If they are being blown into a large holding tank, the air stream may simply blow into the tank and exit from the top, dropping the pellets in the tank. If the destination is too small a container for this, or if it is desired to recirculate the air or to separate fines from the air stream before discharge, then the stream passes into a cyclone separator, which drops the pellets to the container, and the air continues to the next step.

Lobe type blowers are usually used for large systems because they can produce large volumes of air at relatively high pressures, but centrifugal blowers may be adequate on a small line. Fluff transfer lines operate at lower pressure drop than pellet lines, so can be served by centrifugal blowers. Entry air must be filtered to prevent product contamination; this is usually done by bag filters, but screen filters are also used. The air intake must be protected to prevent entry of moisture in bad weather.

The piping is commonly aluminum and should have interior treatment to prevent coating of the interior with polymer. Many polyolefin plastics, when air transferred through a completely smooth surfaced pipe, will smear out a little polymer on the surface each time a pellet impinges on the wall. These little smears gradually build up to a continuous coating which, from time to time, will slough off sections producing what is termed "snake skins". These can be very troublesome in blocking transfer equipment. If the interior of the pipe is roughened in just the right way, the development of the snake skins can be prevented. This generally increases the abrasion of the pellets slightly, but the material worn off is in the form of fines, which cause less trouble than the snake skin. Fluff can be transferred in smooth lines, for it causes no snake skin problems.

Fines Removal   An excessive amount of fine material mixed in with pellets is likely to cause problems in the processing plant. Therefore, pellets that have been air transferred a good deal must be separated from the resulting fines. This is usually accomplished by means of cyclone separators carefully designed to provide particle size separation; these will take the pellets out of the air stream, while maintaining the fines in suspension. The fines are then removed from the air stream by bag filters, and the air is either recompressed to pick up the pellets again or allowed to escape.

Pellets may be transferred in this way for distances up to about a half mile in a continuous pipe. If longer runs are desired it is necessary to have intermediate pumping stations, otherwise the pressure drop is so great that the resulting air expansion produces exit velocities so high as to cause excessive fines production.

Switching of Flow   Flow of material is switched from one branch of a pipeline to another by means of special butterfly valves with resilient seats. The design of these is quite critical because they must close reliably in the presence of relatively large plastics particles which would jam an ordinary valve and prevent its closing. Since different types of resin are frequently handled by the same line, perfect closing of the valves is essential to prevent cross contamination. The valves may be manually operated, but in most plants they are automatically controlled from a central switchboard, which not only operates every valve in the system but also indicates the position of every valve in the plant at all times. This is very important in preventing mistransfer of material.

Control of Atmosphere   Ordinary air is the most commonly used transfer medium in these pipe lines, but in some cases raw resin, especially fluff, contains solvents or may of itself be fine enough to present a dust explosion hazard with air. In such cases nitrogen or carbon dioxide may be used to reduce the oxygen content below the explosive limit. Such systems generally are of the recirculating type to reduce inert gas costs, and generally also provide for inert gas blanketing of all silos, bins, or other containers.

Packing and Shipping

As little as ten years ago the commonest shipping container for polyolefin plastics was a 50 pound multiwall bag. At the present time the largest poundage of polyolefin plastics is shipped in bulk in specially designed rail cars and trucks, with a smaller amount being shipped in 1000 pound corrugated board boxes. The trend to bulk shipment and large containers will undoubtedly continue, because of the resulting reduction in labor costs, both at the producer and consumer end. It also reflects the increased sophistication of the industry, and the tendency towards increased size in the consuming unit.

The bulk shipment of plastic pellets has been made possible by the development of rail cars suitable for this purpose. These are essentially tank cars, but the bottom of the tank is sloped in such a way that pellet resin will empty out completely into an air conveyor system at the bottom. These cars generally have three or four compartments, each with a separate filling opening at the top, and with a separate connection to an air conveyor at the bottom.

At the resin manufacturing plant they are generally filled by gravity flow from a large bin located above the railroad siding, through the top opening. When the car is full, this opening is closed and sealed, and the plastic is then fully protected from any contamination until it arrives at the destination.

When the user receives the car he attaches the bottom connections to his air transfer system and transfers the contents of the car to his raw material bins. It is also possible to transfer directly from the rail car to the processing equipment and this is sometimes done. However, rail demurrage charges are generally high enough to warrant the installation of the needed bins.

QUALITY CONTROL AND TESTING

One of the most important phases of any manufacturing operation is the control of product quality.

Polyolefin plastic resins are generally carefully tailored to some specific end use. It is often very difficult to judge the suitability of a particular lot of material for its end use except by trying it. For this reason specialty resins are actually tested by fabricating an end use type sample and testing it. In most cases end use testing is done only on final lots, but in some plants it starts with periodic checks at the reactor level, and continues at intermediate process steps as well.

Because of the length of time required to make and test a sample, end use testing is not a practical means of routine in-process checking. It is necessary to have some test that can be done quickly to keep track of how the process is going. The most common tests for this purpose are melt index and density; sometimes melt flow ratio or some other test will also be used. These tests were discussed in Chapter 2, Physical Properties. The important feature of these tests is that they may be performed in a few minutes, and while they may have little to do with end product performance, they are a very good indication of how the reaction is progressing, and a change in these properties gives a good clue as to what corrective action is necessary to maintain quality.

In the case of the low pressure methods, control of catalyst quality and raw material purity is also highly essential. In most cases there is no criterion of catalyst quality except how it polymerizes the olefin. In order to check this the control laboratory usually has a small bench reactor which can make a few grams of material under carefully controlled standard conditions. When a new batch of catalyst is received for test, a run is made on this reactor and the amount and quality of resin produced is compared to a standard. Acceptance depends on the result of this comparison. The most critical catalyst poison in the low pressure process is water. The critical amounts are so small that ordinary analytical methods are useless. The best general purpose test is dew point. To measure the dew point at a water level as low as possible, it is necessary to go to cryogenic temperatures with the dew point apparatus.

This chapter has not even touched upon many points connected with polyolefin plastic manufacture but has attempted only a very general overview to give some idea of the nature of the operation and to introduce some concepts and some pieces of equipment essential to understanding the production of these materials.

FIVE

processing polyolefin plastics

MATERIALS HANDLING

The modern polyolefin processing plant receives its resin in bulk by rail car or truck, unloads the material by air conveyor into large silos, and distributes the resin to the individual processing machines pneumatically. Transfer systems may be actuated by compressed air or by vacuum. Very commonly both are used; resin is blown to the bins by compressed air and distributed to the using machines by suction devices, which are actuated by a hopper level sensor at the machine, which draws in resin when the level descends below a preset point. This means that the machine operator does nothing about resin handling but does make the proper piping connections and sees that the automatic equipment operates properly.

Automatic handling equipment not only saves labor involved in resin handling but also helps prevent resin contamination and assures that it arrives at the machine at a uniform temperature.

Coloring and Compounding

There has been an increase in the amount of coloring and compounding of polyolefins done at the resin consuming facility in recent years. This is likely to increase further as plants expand.

Injection molders commonly color polyolefins by blending dry pigments with resin pellets. They also blend linear and high pressure polyethylene pellets to obtain materials intermediate between the two in flexibility.

In the extrusion field there is more of a tendency to use masterbatch for this purpose. A masterbatch is a polyolefin compound containing a high concentration of color or additive; it is mixed with natural resin in the proper proportions before use to give the final mix the desired additive concentration.

In addition to colors, masterbatches may be used in both molding and extrusion to add slip and antiblock to film resins, ultraviolet absorbers to film and monofilament resins, carbon black to pipe resins, butyl rubber or other elastomers to improve the impact strength of the resin, and glass fibers to improve the strength and heat resistance of moldings, as well as other materials for special uses.

The cost of masterbatch and the blending operation is generally lower than the cost of purchasing a premixed compound from the resin manufacturer. This is not, however, the principal incentive for on-plant compounding. The real advantage is the ability to buy and store in bulk a small number of base resins; these may be modified as needed in accordance with a particular order, instead of having to maintain an inventory of a large number of special compounds.

Mixing

On-plant mixing of dry color is usually done in a tumble blender, which may be merely a fiber drum mounted on an axle that may turn end for end or at an angle. Cement mixers may also be used, or, of course, blenders similar to those used at the resin manufacturers plant.

When dry color quality better than that obtained by tumble blending is needed, an intensive dry mixer may be used, as at the manufacturing plant.

Pigment Dispersants

Dry coloring is facilitated by precoating the polymer pellets with mineral oil or other viscous liquids which would stick the pigments to the pellets. This reduces dusting, allows the use of higher pigment loadings, which would not segregate from the pellets during handling, and shortens the needed mixing cycle. Of course, care must be taken to avoid a dispersant that with damage resin quality, and to avoid excessive use that will result in the dispersant bleeding to the surface of the finished product. Dispersants may also, in some cases, cause pigment agglomeration.

Masterbatch Blending

In addition to the types of blenders used for dry color blending, masterbatch is very commonly blended by continuously feeding a stream of masterbatch and a stream of raw resin to the processing equipment. Available equipment can maintain the proportions of the two streams accurately, even when overall rate changes must be made to accommodate the process. Belt feeders that actually perform a continuous weighing are very accurate but expensive. Screw feeders are very satisfactory in most cases; and piston feeders which feed measured volumes are also good, where the materials being fed do not vary appreciably in bulk density. These devices do not actually weigh out product; hence, in order to get proportions by weight, the output must be weighed over a range of conditions to obtain a calibration curve.

SCREW EXTRUDERS

At the present time almost all machines processing polyolefin plastics have a screw extruder, regardless of whether the final processing operation is injection molding, blow molding, or extrusion through a die.

The extruder performs two functions: it melts the plastic pellets, and it delivers the melt under pressure to the forming operation.

There is at present a great deal of activity in the extruder screw design field, and new screw designs are constantly appearing, each claimed to increase output or to improve product quality. Some of these new designs and the advantages to be gained from them will be discussed at the end of this section. However, first we will discuss conventional screw design and the theory that was developed in order to understand it. It should be pointed out that the simplified theory we will discuss is valuable mainly because it clarifies the process, but it is very much limited as a means of performance prediction or extruder design. The most progressive extruder manufacturers now have computer programs, usually based on empirical relations derived from many experiments, which they use for the practical design.

While the original analysis of the operation of a screw pump was made in 1922, it was not until the early fifties that serious work was done to apply it to the extrusion of plastics. Up to that time plastics extruders had been developed strictly on a cut and try basis.

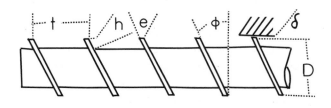

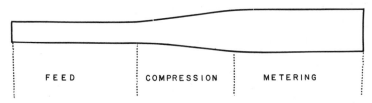

Figure 5.1. Diagram of a polyolefin extruder screw, defining terms used.

A screw extruder consists simply of a helical screw rotated inside a closely fitting cylinder. A kitchen meat grinder is a good example. The plastics extruder differs from this in being longer, having shallower screw flights, and having a heated cylinder. Figure 5.1 shows a typical polyolefin extruder screw, and serves to define some of the terms we will use in the discussion.

Lead (t) is the distance between two successive threads of the screw. In most polyolefin screws it is equal to the screw diameter.

Depth (h) is the distance that the screw thread stands out from the base.

Screw Diameter (D) is the diameter of the cylinder defined by the outer portion of the screw thread.

Root Diameter is the diameter of the cylindrical portion at the base of the threads $(D\text{-}2h)$.

The typical polyolefin extrusion screw has three sections: a relatively deep feed section, a compression section where the depth gradually decreases, and a shallow metering section. While these sections are shown in the illustration as relatively long feed and compression sections, and a shorter metering section, the relative length depends on the application. It is quite common, for instance, to use screws in extrusion coating that consist of half or more metering section; and some screws used for film extrusion are mostly compression section with only a short metering section.

Simplified Flow Theory

This theory applies only to the metering section of an extruder, but since the metering section is shallower than the other portions, it exerts the greatest effect on screw output.

If Q is the output of an extruder, Q_D is drag flow, Q_P the pressure flow and Q_L the leakage flow all in cubic inches per second, then $Q = Q_D - Q_P - Q_L$.

As the screw turns, the land presses against the melt between the lands pushing the melt in a direction perpendicular to the land. Since the land is at an angle to the axis of rotation this motion may be considered to have two parts, a transverse component which merely pushes it around the barrel, and an axial component which pushes it down the barrel. This last component is the drag flow Q_D.

At the end of the extruder there is a die, or other restriction which resists the flow, and so a pressure builds up. This pressure also pushes back along the screw channel, producing a flow backward up the channel. This is the pressure flow Q_P.

The screw does not fit into the cylinder exactly, but there must always be a little clearance between the cylinder and the end of the land. Some melt leaks back through this small space. This is Q_L, the leakage flow. In any reasonably well fitted extruder Q_L is negligible.

If N is the screw rotational speed in revolutions per second, ϕ the helix angle of the land, P the pressure difference across the metering section, μ the viscosity of the melt, and L the length of the metering section, then it can be shown that:

$$Q_D = \frac{\pi^2 D^2 N h \sin \phi \cos \phi}{2}$$

and

$$Q_p = \frac{\pi h^3 D \sin^2 \phi P}{12 \mu L}$$

The main assumptions made in this theory are:

(1) The metering section determines flow.
(2) Leakage flow is negligible.
(3) Viscosity is constant.
(4) Flow is Newtonian.
(5) Land width is negligible compared to channel width.
(6) A single flight screw is used.

In any actual case (3) and (4) are probably the largest sources of error and also the most difficult to correct for. Even if we understand that we will not get an exact value from these equations, we can use them to see what factors will affect the extruder output.

N appears only in the drag flow, so if everything else is held constant, output is directly proportional to screw speed.

P appears only in the pressure flow, so an increase in pressure at the end of the screw reduces output.

D appears squared in Q_D but only to the first power in Q_p. Therefore, output increases as the square of the extruder diameter at low pressures, but as pressure increases the output increases at some value less than the square of the diameter.

"h" appears in Q_D only as the first power, but cubed in Q_p. This means that the output of a deeply cut screw is very pressure sensitive, but that of a shallow screw is quite insensitive to pressure differences.

μ appears only in the Q_p formula and then in the denominator, so the higher the viscosity the greater the flow at constant pressure, or the flow is less sensitive to pressure differences at higher viscosities.

L appears only in the denominator of the Q_p formula, so longer metering sections give more output at a given pressure and are less pressure sensitive than short metering sections.

Considering the pertinent factors in any individual case makes it

possible to decide on what changes to make in screw design or operation to achieve a particular objective. Relatively small changes made
by consideration of this theory will generally be in the right direction, although they may not be quantitatively correct.

Velocity Distribution in the Screw Channel   Melt does not flow
down the channel in a uniform stream, but moves forward mainly
near the barrel surface. This can be understood as follows. If we
take velocity profiles down through the material in the grooves of
the screw, we find that drag flow is proportional to the distance from
the screw root surface as shown in Figure 5.2.

Pressure flow, however has a profile like Figure 5.3.

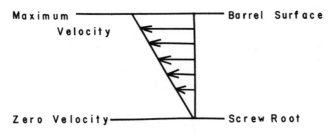

Figure 5.2. Drag flow velocity profile in a screw thread.

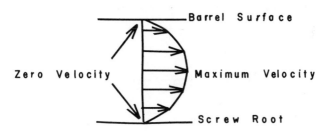

Figure 5.3. Pressure flow velocity profile in a screw
thread.

If we put the two together we get a net flow that might look like
Figure 5.4.

This shows us a lot about how an extruder works; it shows that the
bottom of a deep flight contributes little to forward flow, if there is
appreciable back pressure. This is why modern extruder screws, es-

pecially in the metering section where this theory applies, are quite shallow.

We also can see one of the mixing actions in the screw; the difference in forward velocity at various depths brings materials that entered the screw at different times out together. This forward velocity by itself, however, would lead us to some mistaken ideas, because we would assume that material would just lie at the bottom of the groove, or even go backward, which ordinarily does not happen.

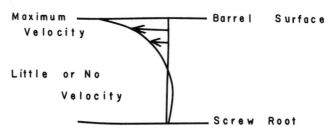

Figure 5.4. Combined flow in a screw thread.

We spoke earlier of the transverse component of the drag flow without discussing its effect. This does not contribute to forward flow but it contributes greatly to mixing. The transverse component establishes a flow across the screw groove. When this flow gets to the land on the far side of the groove, it pushes downward and so establishes a flow pattern that turns the entire contents of the screw over and over (see Figure 5.5).

Figure 5.5. Transverse flow in a screw thread.

This prevents stagnation at the screw root and is another important mixing action.

Heat Generation in the Extruder Screw   In addition to the forwarding and mixing actions, the extruder also has the very important function of melting the plastic. While melting as such is complete before the metering section, one very important fact about heat generation in an extruder can be understood from the illustrations of flow in the metering section. Some of the heat for melting comes by conduction through the barrel, but by far the greatest amount of heat comes from shearing within the plastic. Shearing results from the difference in speed of adjacent layers of material. We have seen that drag and pressure flow result in high velocity near the barrel, which drops off sharply with depth. It is in this region of large velocity differences between layers that heat generation is greatest. We also have seen that in the transverse flow this material at the barrel surface flows to the land, then down to the screw root. This results in hotter material at all the metal-plastic interfaces, surrounding a core of colder material which is only very gradually heated by conduction from the hot material. It is, therefore, necessary to have a very long flow path before a uniform temperature is obtained.

In the study of flow, the amount of leakage over the top of the land is considered negligible. The heat generation in this location, however, is not negligible. The small clearance in this area results in extremely high rates of shear, and, consequently, in a high rate of heat generation. This small amount of very hot material enters the main flow at the barrel surface with the material heated at the highest rate of shear, adding to the temperature difference in the material.

Melting in the Extruder   There has recently been a good deal of work done on the melting of the plastic in the compression section, before the mass is entirely molten. In this region flow patterns are quite different from those in the metering section. What happens here is that there is initially a mass of solid resin. This is melted at the barrel face by a combination of heat conduction and the high rate of shear in this area. The transverse and drag flows move this molten material over to the "pushing" land where it accumulates, forcing the remaining unmelted material forward to the leading land. This is schematically shown in Figure 5.6.

Figure 5.6. Plastic melting in the compression section.

As the compression section groove depth decreases, the solid material is pushed up against the barrel surface, melting more and more of it until it is all molten. Generally, well before it is all melted, the drag of the viscous melt begins to break up the solid mass. Thus, except in a very shallow screw, it is quite possible for the transverse flow pattern typical of the metering section to be established with solid particles present in the cooler center core of the groove.

It has recently been shown that certain polyolefin resins can suffer considerable damage from being extruded in machines with improperly designed feed sections. The materials in question are high molecular weight materials, used for applications where long life is essential, such as in cable sheathings. If such materials are extruded under conditions where unmelted pellets may be advanced to such restricted portions of the compression section that the solid is subjected to direct shear between the screw root and the cylinder, then reduction in melt index, stress crack resistance, and service life will occur. It is assumed that this results in small areas of extremely high temperature, which damages the resin. Damage of this sort can be reduced by the use of long and very gradual compression sections. The conventional feed section may be eliminated entirely, with the screw consisting only of a compression section and a metering section. Study of melting in the screw has also shown that such screws have a somewhat greater melting capacity than conventional screws.

Limitations of Conventional Screw Design   It can be seen from this discussion that the conventional extruder screw as described is not a very efficient means of obtaining a melt of uniform temperature. In order to assure complete melting, it is necessary to heat part of the melt well above the average temperature needed. This is undesirable for two reasons: first, all of the polyolefins deteriorate if heated too hot, so that damage to the resin is increased by the need for higher temperature; and secondly because extruder production is reduced by the need for higher temperatures. Two factors limit production: the extruder has only a limited heating capacity, hence the hotter the melt the less output; also, whatever process the extruder is feeding, it is necessary to cool the melt to make the final product. Very often the cooling capacity of the end product process limits system output, so the hotter the melt the lower the output.

In addition to this, the melt delivered by the screw will vary in temperature from one part to another. This prevents uniform extrusion from the die which follows.

Recent Developments in Extruder Screw Design   The problems with the conventional extruder screw, mentioned in the previous paragraph, have resulted in a number of new screw designs which mix the melt in the screw to obtain a more uniform melt temperature and to prevent the passage of unmelted resin. These have taken two general forms, pins in the groove and melt overflow dams. The devices called pins are not really what most people would call pins, since they are wider than they are long. They are short cylindrical studs placed closely together in the screw channel in various configurations, many of which are patented. One commonly used configuration is a circle of studs all the way around an extruder screw, at right angles to the axis. Another is a row of studs from one land to the next, parallel to the axis. Single rows or as many as three or four parallel rows with pins staggered from each other in adjacent rows may be used (see Figure 5.7).

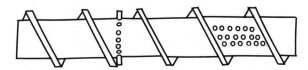

Figure 5.7. Some pin arrangements used in an extruder screw.

The studs are generally placed at the start of the metering section, but may also be placed at or near the end of the metering section. Spacing is generally quite close, with 20-50 mils between studs, and the stud is from $\frac{1}{4}$-$\frac{1}{2}$ inch in diameter. The ends of the studs may conform as closely to the barrel as the top of the land, or may be 10 mils or more shorter. Passage between the pins mixes the melt, and the narrow spaces screen out any solid particles.

Melt overflow dams may be placed in similar locations, but most designs provide for a longer overflow length to allow a narrower clearance without building up excessive pressures. One of the first such designs was the Maileffer screw. In this design a second screw flight was started, branching off from the main flight and in a half dozens turns gradually crossing the groove to intersect the other side of the flight, thus forcing all of the melt to flow between the top of the flight and the barrel. A similar result is produced by means of a mixing section with staggered grooves. Half of the grooves start at the upstream end of the mixing section and dead end near the downstream end. The grooves between these start a little past the upstream end and open out into the downstream end, thereby forcing all the melt to flow over the raised portion of the mixing section between the grooves. In any case the melt is forced through a clearance of 15-30 mils, holding back any unmelted particles and mixing melt from various portions of the original extruder groove, to give a homogeneous melt. Like the studs these dams may be placed at the start of the metering section or at its end.

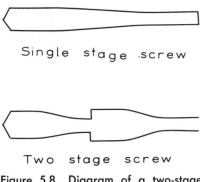

Single stage screw

Two stage screw

Figure 5.8. Diagram of a two-stage screw showing root diameter only.

When properly sized for the particular resin used, any of these devices, with a suitable screw, can produce a homogeneous melt at higher rates and at a lower temperature than could be produced from a conventional screw. At this time experience with them is too limited to say which design is preferable for a particular situation, but it it appears probable that most screws will incorporate some such feature in the future.

Another special screw type that has been finding increasing application is the two stage screw. This type of screw has two feed sections, two compression sections, and two metering sections. The diagrams in Figure 5.8 represent the root cylinder of the screws only, that is, the flights are not shown, in order to make the nature of the screws clearer. The upper figure represents a conventional one stage screw. In order to make the differences in flight depth visible, these diagrams are grossly out of scale.

Two stage screws may be used with a vent to the atmosphere or to a vacuum in the second feeding section to remove volatiles from the melt. Two stage screws used without the vent may provide better homogenization than a single stage screw. Two stage screws are particularly useful for the extrusion of powdered resin. The polyolefins produced by the low pressure process are originally obtained in the form of small granules. These are sometimes called fluff or flake. They are ordinarily processed into pellets for use in final processing operations. Two stage extruders are useful for this purpose when used with a vent, because the fluff may contain a little solvent or moisture. It is also possible to process the fluff directly into a final product. While this can sometimes be done in conventional extruders, in many cases a two stage extruder will give a better product.

Another type of screw that has recently been recommended for polyolefins is called the five zone screw. It differs from the conventional screw only in that the compression zone is in two stages with a zone of uniform depth between. The first compression zone assures an early build-up of pressure and temperature, which facilitates the removal of air and volatiles in the rear. The uniform depth zone provides homogenization without further heat build-up. This screw is claimed to give good quality extrudate at higher outputs than a conventional screw (see Figure 5.9).

Figure 5.9. Diagram of five-zone screw.

Power Consumption in an Extruder   As with simplified flow theory dealing with output, it is necessary to make so many simplifying assumptions to obtain a workable formula for power consumption that its use in a practical calculation is doubtful, but as a qualitative means of understanding the process, it is extremely valuable.

Using the same notation as was used for the flow equation, and introducing three new terms: δ the clearance between the land and the barrel, e the width of the land and $\bar{\mu}$ the average viscosity, we can derive an equation for Z, the power requirement. It is as follows:

$$Z = \frac{\pi^3 D^3 N^2}{h} L \bar{\mu} + \frac{Q_D P}{\cos^2 \phi} + \frac{\pi^2 D^2 N^2 e}{\delta \tan \phi} L \bar{\mu}$$

The far right hand group of symbols represents the power consumption of the material between the barrel and the top of the land. Since the clearance δ is very small, it can readily be seen that this factor can be quite large. In fact a calculation will show that this may be several times as large as the two other factors combined. This is the largest source of error in this calculation, because the large power consumption in this location makes the assumption of any kind of average viscosity impossible. There is only a very small amount of material in this space, so the power consumed heats it up very rapidly, giving it a much lower viscosity than the rest of the polymer. In addition the shear rate in this space is very much higher than elsewhere. All the polyolefins have shear sensitive viscosities, so the viscosity is further reduced by the high shear rate. This means that the effective viscosity in this part of the formula is very much smaller than that elsewhere in the formula, so the heat production, while still important, is not as large a factor as it appears to be. While these facts reduce the value of the formula for calculation, they do not change the qualitative value for understanding.

The first qualitative conclusion is implied above, and that is, if so much power is absorbed in the space between land and barrel, then a small amount of material is heated much more than the rest, resulting in the uneven temperature previously discussed, and also in the possibility of deteriorating resin due to overheating. One expedient that can be used to combat this is to increase δ, that is to use a loosely fitting screw. However, to be very effective, a clearance of 8 or 10 mils would have to be used, and this would decrease the pumping efficiency of the screw, so this is not very useful. Since this material is directly adjacent to the wall of the barrel, it is possible to cool it by conduction, and barrel cooling in the metering section is commonly used. Making the land width e as small as practical is also useful. Since N, the screw speed, is squared in this expression, lower screw speed will reduce the heating.

Regarding screw speed, notice that it appears squared in two of the expressions in the power formula, but that it appears only in the first power in the drag flow formula. This means that as screw speed is increased, to increase output, the power consumption, and thus the heat produced, goes up much faster than the output, and melt temperature will increase. If melt temperature must be kept down, this limits the allowable screw speed. On the other hand, of course, if melting capacity is the limitation, then higher screw speed helps.

The center expression in the power formula shows another source of melt temperature control: pressure. Increasing pressure increases power consumption and stock temperature, and this can be used as an important means of melt temperature control. Any polyolefin extruder used in service, where high melt temperatures are needed, should be equipped with a valve in the adaptor to permit control of back pressure; on the other hand, where low melt temperatures are desired, back pressure should be kept as low as possible.

Also L, which does not appear at all in the drag flow formula, appears in two of the three power expressions, so it can be seen that the longer the screw the greater the power consumption for a given output, and the greater the resulting stock temperature.

The screw diameter also appears differently in flow and power formulas. It appears cubed in one, and squared in another of the power expressions. It appears squared in the drag flow formula but also in the opposing pressure flow formula in the first power. The exact balance of these factors will differ in various cases but, in general, the larger diameter machine will produce a higher temperature melt at the same speed of rotation.

A useful formula for estimating the power required for an extruder is derived from the fact that most modern extruders are operated essentially adiabatically. That is to say, there is no net inflow or outflow of heat through the barrel, so that all the heat has to be produced from the power input to the screw. Since the polymer leaving the extruder die has essentially no kinetic energy, and is at atmospheric pressure, it is only necessary to calculate the amount of heat gained by the polymer and convert that into power.

The polymer absorbs heat in two ways: by melting and by increasing in temperature. If H is the heat of fusion in BTU/lb, $\triangle T$ the difference in temperature between the polymer entering the machine and that leaving it, C the average heat capacity in BTU/lb °F, W the throughput of the machine in lb/hr, and Z the horsepower required, then:

$$Z = 3.9 \times 10^{-4} \, W(C\Delta T + H)$$

Some extruders are cooled a good deal while operating. If there is any considerable heat removal, this must, of course, be added to the power requirement.

Extruder Scale-up   The preceding discussion points up many of the problems that arise when you try to get more output from a machine. When you need a high temperature melt, there is no problem, except that the larger machine will consume disproportionately more power. When the melt temperature must be limited, scale-up is a serious problem, and there is really no completely satisfactory answer. The compromise that has to be made is to make the machine larger, but to run it slower to keep the temperature down. Also, quite commonly larger machines are made proportionally shorter.

The first work on simplified flow theory indicated that two geometrically similar isothermal extruders should produce the same die pressure, and that their outputs and power consumption will be in the ratio of the cubes of the diameter if rotational speed is the same. Some work was done verifying this relation, but, in fact, it has proved of little value in scale-up because the larger machine would produce a much less homogeneous melt if operated at the same screw speed, and no plastics extruder can operate even nearly isothermally.

A common scale-up formula that applies to polyolefins is the following. If the ratio of the scaled-up machine diameter to that of the smaller model is F, then all dimensions of the small extruder are multiplied by F to give the corresponding dimension of the larger extruder, except groove depth, which is multiplied by the square root of F. The machine is then operated at a speed $1/F$ of that of the model. This is a purely empirical formula, but experience shows that it generally gives a practical large machine. The output of the large machine is about $F^{1.5}$ times that of the smaller. Many people consider this formula to be too conservative and prefer the following formula:

$$h = h_0 \, (D/D_0)^{.75}$$
$$n = n_0 \, (D_0/D)^{.75}$$

Here h is the groove depth of the scaled-up extruder, h_o that of the model, n the speed of the scaled-up extruder, n_o that of the model, and D and D_o the respective diameters. This gives the large extruder a greater groove depth, and operates it at a higher speed than the previous formula, so it has a greater output for a given diameter ratio. The exponent used varies with different materials, but .75 is a reasonable value for polyolefins under ordinary conditions. This gives the larger machine an output about the square of the diameter ratio times that of the smaller, if all other screw dimensions are increased by the diameter ratio. This works well at small scale-up ratios, but at large ratios the large machine will generally produce a hotter melt.

Extruder Drives   Most extruders are operated under conditions requiring control of the output rate and are, therefore, driven by a variable speed drive. For small machines the usual means of speed variation is to use mechanical double cone speed changers. In these machines a stiff, wide Vee belt is operated between two pulleys that consist of two cones, which can be pulled apart or pushed together. If the cones are pulled apart, the belt rides nearer the shaft, making the pulley smaller, while if the cones are pushed together, the belt rides higher. By synchronizing the motion of the moveable cones, considerable speed variation is possible.

These drives are inexpensive, efficient, and the torque available increases as speed decreases, which is what an extruder requires. However, wear is rapid, so frequent maintenance becomes a problem, and this becomes increasingly serious as the size of the drive increases. For this reason these drives are usually limited to below 40 horsepower.

Traditionally the variable speed DC motor has been the ideal extruder drive; however, as its use entails the conversion of AC to DC, it is quite expensive. These drives are efficient; they can be made with torque characteristics of any desired nature and give long, maintenance-free service.

A variety of new drive systems has been developed in order to get some of the advantages of the DC drive at lower cost, and for many applications AC variable speed motors are now available. They do not, in general, have the excellent torque characteristics of the DC motor, and in some cases, the solid state circuitry used is

difficult for operators' servicemen to understand, making main-
tnance dependent on factory service.

One very satisfactory drive for the common case where an extruder will generally be operated at some predetermined speed, but
requiring the ability to slow down for short times, is the magnetic
clutch drive. In this drive a watercooled magnetic clutch can be set
to slip at a certain rate to reduce the speed of the extruder relative
to that of the primary drive. These drives are by no means a simple
slip clutch, but can produce a controlled speed reduction by control
of the eddy currents produced by the relative motion of the plates.
They are, however, inefficient at high reductions, because the speed
is reduced by wasting the excess power, and there is no torque increase as speed decreases. This limits their application.

An increasing number of extruders is being equipped with hydraulic drives. These are especially suitable for service where the
screw is started and stopped frequently, as in an injection molding
machine. The small size and light weight of the hydraulic drive
motor makes it particularly suitable for situations where the operation of the machine requires the drive to move back and forth. Since
the hydraulic drive motors can be made for low rotational speeds,
they can be directly connected to the screw without the reduction
gears required by electric motors. Hydraulic drive motors are also
very useful in hazardous locations, where the lack of electrical connections and potential spark hazard is valuable. Another place where
they excel is in services, where the speed changes of the extruder
have to be synchronized very accurately with speed changes in a
long train of other equipment. In this case all the drives can be run
from a single hydraulic pump, and when the pump speed is changed,
the entire train will change simultaneously. In spite of their excellent
characteristics, their high cost limits use to special situations.

POLYOLEFIN FILM PRODUCTION

The Blown Film Process

Most low density polyethylene film is made by the blown film process. It is also possible to make film from other polyolefins in this
way, but the resulting films are generally not of a commercial
quality, so for all practical purposes, it is a process for making low
density polyethylene film.

In this process a tube of molten polyethylene is extruded from a circular die and is expanded by internal air pressure while it is still molten to form a very thin walled tube. It is then cooled, the tube collapsed and slit to give a single film. It can also be rolled up without slitting, as tubular film.

While there are many variations of this process, the basic equipment needed can be well understood from Figure 5.10, which shows a small commercial blown film unit.

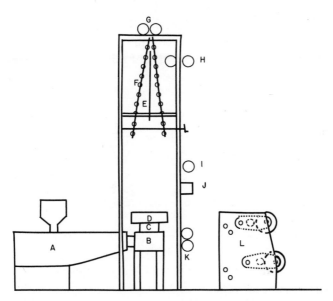

Figure 5.10. Blown film equipment. A. Extruder. B. Rotator. C. Die. D. Air ring. E. Gusseting assembly. F. Collapsers. G. Upper nip rolls. H. Treater assembly. I. Wrinkle remover. J. Trimmer and slitter. K. Lower nip rolls. L. Winder.

The essential elements of this unit, following material flow from the extruder, are the die, air ring, gusseting frame, collapsing frame, nip rolls, treater, slitters, trimmer, lower nip rolls, and winder. Each of these elements will be discussed in this order, explaining major variations and the reasons for them.

Blown Film Dies Most modern blown film dies are rotated. The reason for this is that some thickness variation in the extruded tube cannot be avoided. This variation can be kept to the point where, in itself, it is not objectionable, but if the die and other elements of the assembly are stationary, then the thicker sections of the tube pile on top of each other in successive laps of the finished roll and produce high spots. When it is considered that a roll may consist of 5000 or more layers of film, then it is clear that even a very small thickness difference may produce a high spot of serious proportions on the roll. The film on the outside of the roll is then no longer flat, but buckles as it is unrolled and becomes unmanageable in subsequent converting operations. If the die is rotated, the high spots do not come on top of each other, but are distributed evenly across the roll, making a perfectly smooth roll.

In order to make rotation possible, the melt entry must be through the bottom of the die, through a rotating joint. The most common die design for this purpose is shown in Figure 5.11.

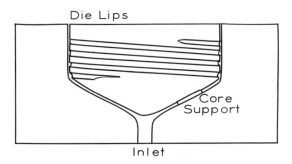

Figure 5.11. Spider-type blown film die.

This is called a spider die because the center core pin is supported by several (usually three) short arms which connect it to the main die body through the plastic flow channel. These arms are usually streamlined in shape, and as small as possible to avoid interference with polymer flow. In spite of this, the flow disturbance caused by them will cause an appearance defect in the film, unless provisions are made to smooth it out in the flow passage above the obstruction. One of the most successful means of accomplishing this is to put several shallow spiral grooves around the core pin in the part defining the narrow vertical flow channel. This tends to split the polymer flow into two parts: that moving vertically, and that moving around the spirals. This causes enough mixing to obliterate the defects in the film.

Another bottom-fed die is the internal channel type (Figure 5.12). In this case the center core is fitted directly to the base of the die body, and the polymer enters a central vertical channel in the core, which branches out into horizontal channels, which distribute polymer to the annular die opening. This kind of die has the advantage that the pressure of the polymer melt entering the die is not exerted over the entire core area, as in the spider type, but only on the much smaller channel area. This is important in the case of large dies, where it permits the use of lighter construction. Dies of this sort also produce film appearance defects, where the adjacent flow streams merge, so similar means must be used to mix the flow.

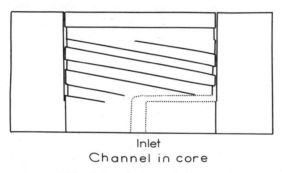

Inlet
Channel in core

Figure 5.12. Internal channel blown film die.

Many other types of dies are used, including side-fed dies which can not be rotated. These may be used on units where other means of distributing the high spots are used. Such means will be discussed later.

Very large dies, which may be used to make film 20 or up to 60 feet wide are generally not rotated. Such film is generally folded back on itself several times before making a roll, so there is no problem with high spot formation. Also, since this kind of film is used on construction projects or for agricultural uses, there is no problem with subsequent converting.

Air Rings When the hot tube of plastic emerges from the die it is inflated up to the desired size by air pressure. A passage for air pressure must be provided through the die core for this purpose. At the same time it is cooled by a current of air blown on the outside by an air ring. This air ring also usually is rotated, sometimes by direct connection to the die, and sometimes independently. Figure 5.13 shows a commercial air ring designed for independent rotation.

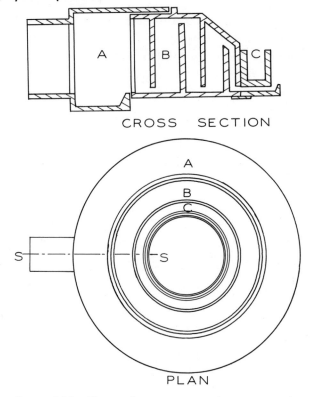

CROSS   SECTION

PLAN

Figure 5.13. Plan and cross section of an air ring for
blown film. A. Stationary duct. B. Rotating baffle rings.
C. Adjustable inserts.

Air enters this ring through a stationary manifold which encircles
the ring. The complex internal baffling shown in the cross section is
for distributing the air evenly around the tube. Air exits at the
inner face of this ring, which surrounds the plastic tube. This air
ring has removable inner sections, which can be changed for use on
different sizes of film. The horizontal air exit passage has a lip at
the end which turns the air stream upward, so that it flows parallel
to the tube rather than impinging on it directly. This is to prevent
distortion and fluttering of the tube, which is very soft and weak at
this point.

Gusseting Frame   When film is to be used as tubular film to
make bags, it is often desirable to gusset the tube. This means that
instead of simply being flattened by the nip rolls, a portion of the

tube has been tucked in so that it folds in between the main tube layers. See Figure 5.14, which shows an end view of a cut piece of tube, A without gusset, B with gusset.

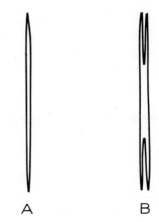

Figure 5.14. End view of gusseted tubing.

A   B

This makes it easier to open the resulting bag, and also makes the bag easier to fill. Deep gussets may be used in wide film to make it possible to roll it up in a narrower roll. The gusseting frame consists of the means for holding and adjusting a gusseting plate on each side of the tube. This plate pushes a portion of the bubble in, at the same time that the collapsing frame is flattening it out, so that when it reaches the nip roller, the film layers are in proper alignment to produce gussetted film (see Figure 5.15).

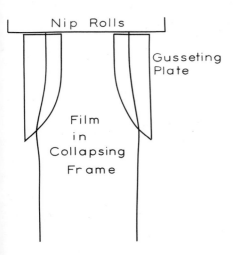

Figure 5.15. Gusseting plate.

Collapsing Frame   The collapsing frame pushes the sides of the bubble together so that they can be flattened by the nip rolls without wrinkles. In the illustration a series of small rollers is shown. This is a very common form. Another common form is a series of wooden slats, and perforated metal is also used. In case of collapsers that do not roll, it is necessary to have them very smooth to avoid scratching the film. Some kind of coating is common to reduce friction, but if the coating is too slippery there will be loss of bubble control. Fluorocarbon polymer coatings, once quite popular, have been largely abandoned for this reason. Various waxes are now more common.

The frame is so arranged that the angle between the two sides is adjustable to accommodate different tube diameters.

The Upper Nip Rolls   The upper nip rolls pinch the tube together to trap the air in the bubble. It should be understood that the uniform size of the bubble, which is essential to good film width control is achieved by trapping a volume of air in the bubble. Air is added through the air inlet tube only to change the bubble size. Under proper conditions of operation the bubble size will remain constant for long periods without further air addition. This means that the nip rolls must be resilient enough to close the bubble completely, without at the same time pinching the edges of the tube so severely as to weaken the creases. The usual practice is to use one steel roll and one rubber covered roll, both of fairly large diameter, usually over 6 inches. The nip rolls must have a means for adjusting the pressure between them to compensate for different film thickness, and should also be arranged to open for convenience in stringing up the unit.

The nip rolls regulate the film speed. Since average film thickness is controlled by balancing extruder output and film speed, it is necessary to have a variable speed drive on the rolls that will maintain a constant speed once the proper setting has been determined.

Some blown film units are equipped with a take-up at the nip roll level, but the common practice is to bring the film down from the nip to the extruder level as shown in Figure 5.10, because this allows one operator to take care of both extruder and take-up.

One reason for having the take-up at the upper level is that this permits the use of a rotating take-up. The same roll smoothing function described under rotating dies can be accomplished by a stationary die and a rotating take-up. In this system the whole assembly of collapsing frame, nip roll, and film take-up is mounted on a platform which can be rotated slowly about an axis directly above the center of the die while the unit is running. While this becomes cumbersome on large units, it is quite satisfactory on relatively small ones.

Film Treaters   Polyolefin films cannot be printed in their natural state, so that any film intended for printing must be given a special treatment. This process is not specific to blown film, but it is discussed at this point because it is a usual feature of a blown film line.

The usual method of treating polyolefin film is to play a corona discharge produced by a high voltage, high frequency electrical arc over the surface of the film. In order to do this the film is led over an insulated, grounded roller, while a high voltage is produced in an electrode close above the film. The high voltage ionizes the air in the gap, allowing a corona discharge to take place through the gap. The electrical current does not actually penetrate through the film and the roll insulation, but these act as the insulation in a capacitor, so that the discharge occurs without direct current flow.

The exact nature of the treatment has not been fully explained. Infrared spectrographic examination of the surface shows that there has been some surface oxidation, and it is believed that the polar groups produced serve as attachments for the ink. Microscopic examination shows that the surface of the film has been covered with minute pits. It is possible that these pits provide the anchor points. It can also be shown that the wetting tension of the surface has been increased, permitting it to be more readily wetted. However, it has also been shown that printability can be induced in polyolefin films by means that produce none of the above phenomena. This has led some researchers to believe that the really significant effect of the treatment is to produce a cross-linked film surface which provides a stable anchorage for ink. Corona treatment is known to produce cross-linking, and if treatment is too severe, it may advance to the point where the plastic is no longer thermoplastic and cannot be heat sealed.

Slitters and Trimmers   While a good deal of blown film is used directly in the form of tubing, any general purpose line must have provision for producing single thickness film, and slit tubes of various configurations.

When single films are required, the tube is generally made slightly oversized and the edges trimmed to remove the edge folds. Other modifications are U tubing, which is made by cutting through both tube layers at one location, and J tubing, which cuts through the two tube layers at different locations.

Lower Nip Rolls   A lower nip roll is not essential to the operation of the line, but it greatly facilitates the slitting and trimming operations by providing a means of tension control independent of roll winding tension. The lower nip rolls are similar to the upper and are driven by a variable speed drive, the speed of which is controlled by a feedback mechanism from a film tension sensor somewhere between the two sets of nip rolls.

Winders   The winders on a blown film line ordinarily have two roll stations, so that the two layers of slit tube can be rolled up on separate rolls. The winders must be able to control winding tension accurately in order to produce a good roll. Rolls may be wound with constant tension, which means that the tension on the film is the same when the roll starts as it is when the roll is finished. As the roll increases in size, the torque on the core increases if the film tension remains constant. This increase in torque may induce slippage in the film layers near the core, and cause telescoping rolls. To prevent this, tension may be reduced as the roll grows to maintain a constant torque on the core. On a large roll constant torque winding may be too hard near the core and too loose at the outside of the roll. For this reason it is common to control roll tensions with some degree of "taper" intermediate between constant tension and constant torque.

Edge Control and Wrinkle Control   There are several ways by which film is kept wrinkle free and accurately aligned. Wrinkles may be removed by bowed rubber rollers, slat expanders, or by edge rollers. Edge control, which assures that the edges of the roll of film will be smooth and square, is accomplished by having edge sensors, usually pneumatic, which activate rollers to correct any movement of the edge of the film away from its predetermined location.

Film Thickness Control It has been customary in blown film manufacture to measure the finished film thickness with a micrometer, and to make take-up speed adjustments by hand in order to bring it to the desired thickness. As the size of units increased, the waste produced by this method has become a serious cost. There are now film thickness gages, generally based on the back-scattering of beta rays, which may be placed against the film bubble to determine its thickness continuously while it is being produced. These gages are at present still used in conjunction with hand adjustments, but by giving an earlier reading they greatly reduce scrap. It is possible to connect these gages to a control mechanism to maintain gage automatically, and this has been done in a few cases, although it is not generally considered economically attractive at the present time.

Chill Roll Cast Film

The chill roll casting method is the second most used method of making polyethylene film, and is also widely used for polypropylene and for multilayer films of various polyolefins or polyolefins and other resins. Multilayer films will be discussed under laminations. In the chill cast method the polyolefin melt is extruded down through a straight slit die, and dropped onto a highly polished, plated roll, which is cooled by internal fluid circulation. The film solidifies on the roll, is stripped off either by another cooled roll or by a neutral roll, and is then trimmed, treated if desired, and rolled up.

This method makes clearer polyethylene film than the blown method. It also makes good film from polypropylene, but polypropylene makes a very poor looking film by the blown process. The chill cast method generally gives better thickness control than the blown film method.

The chill cast process operates at much higher linear speeds than the blown film process, 1800-2000 fpm not being unusual. Blown film is generally limited to about 200 fpm, except for extremely thin (under 0.5 mil) film, which may operate up to twice that. High speed operation requires very sophisticated control equipment and, of course, the necessary cooling capacity on the rolls. As a result, a cast film line is much more expensive than a blown film line, and in spite of the high speeds, the cost of a plant with the same total output is about the same for both methods.

The general design of a casting line is shown in Figure 5.16.

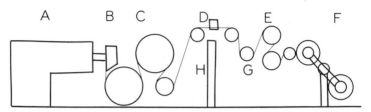

Figure 5.16.   Chill cast film line. A. Extruder. B. Die. C. Chill rolls. D. Trimmer. E. Pull rolls. F. Winder. G. Balance roll. H. Trim disposal.

Briefly, it consists of an extruder, a die, the chill rolls, trimmers, slitters, pull rolls, and a winder.

Dies for the Chill Roll Process   A straight slit die is used for this process, the slit width being generally 15-20 mils, and the length a little longer than the finished width required of the film.

Many die designs are used, but they can be divided into two general types: manifold dies and coathanger dies. In a manifold die a relatively large channel of uniform cross section runs the length of the die, and a narrow slot runs off from one side of this channel to feed the die lips. In a coathanger die a tapered channel runs from the center feed opening down towards each die lip at a slight angle, so that the distance from the channel to the lips decreases towards the edge of the die; a narrow slit runs from this channel to the die lips, but in this case the length of the slit is much shorter at the ends of the die, thus equalizing the pressure drop between the center and the edge portions (see Figure 5.17).

The design of a coathanger die is more critical than that of a manifold die, but if properly designed it can give better control of film thickness. In either type of die the final control of film thickness is by adjustable die lips. Die lip adjustment may be accomplished either by flexing of a thin lip portion of the die body, or by movement of a separate die lip blade on one or both sides of the final die slot. Movement of the lip is produced by a series of bolts that can either push or pull on the lip, depending on which way they are turned. As with blown film, the over-all thickness is controlled by the relative speed of extruder and web. The die adjustment is used only to give a uniform thickness across the web.

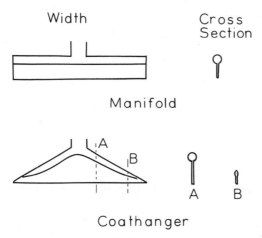

Coathanger

Figure 5.17. Manifold and coathanger die passages.

Chill Rolls   One or more fluid cooled chill rolls may be used. The thinnest possible wall and high fluid velocities are necessary to obtain good heat transfer and uniform roll temperature. The surface finish of the roll determines the surface quality of the film, so a mirror finish chrome plating is usually used. To attain high linear speeds it is necessary to provide some means of preventing air entrapment between the web and the roll. This may consist of air pressure on the film or suction on the roll side. The first roll must be large enough in diameter to solidify the melt before it is stripped from the roll; later rolls are used only to bring the film down to room temperature.

Trimmers and Slitters   The drawdown of the molten plastic between the die lip and the chill roll causes narrowing of the web and the formation of a slight thickening or "bead" at the edge. This bead must be trimmed off before the film is wound up, or the resulting roll will have a high edge. This edge trim constitutes a steady source of scrap in this method, which has no equivalent in the blown film process. The trim scrap is generally removed by suction, chopped into fine flakes, and returned directly to the extruder feed hopper.

Chill cast film is generally made quite wide, six to ten feet wide being typical. It is usually used as a wrapping material for packages requiring widths of one or two feet. In some installations a large "mill roll" is made on the line and slit later, but most modern installations slit in line and wind up rolls of finished width.

Pull Rolls   The tension of the web is determined by a set of pull rolls following the trimmer. The chill rolls themselves determine the speed of the line, and the pull roll speed may be controlled by a web tension sensor or by a manually set differential between pull roll speed and chill roll speed. Pull rolls are generally rubber covered and pull the film by means of an "S" wrap, rather than by pinching it between the rolls as in blown film.

Winders   Winders are generally similar to those used in the blown film process, except that because of the higher linear speeds, they must be more sophisticated in design. They must have automatic roll changers capable of high speed roll change, and very sensitive tension controls to maintain the desired tension at high speeds. In case of units making finished rolls in line the entire roll change sequence is automated with core changers, and roll change is made automatically at a preset footage; the operator only has to remove and label the finished rolls.

Water Bath Film

In the water bath process the same sort of slit die is used as for chill cast film. The web, however, is drawn directly into a tank of cold water, rather than being dropped on a chill roll. With this exception the two processes are quite similar. The water bath method is used for linear polyethylene, polypropylene, and other polyolefins. It may also be used for multilayered films. It is particularly useful for linear polyethylene because the level of the water can be brought quite close to the die lips, causing a very sudden chilling of the melt. This appears to be necessary to produce good optical qualities in linear film.

Film Orientation

For reasons explained under physical properties it is often advantageous to orient polyolefin films. There are two types of orientation, monoaxial and biaxial. Orientation is accomplished by stretching the film at some temperature above room temperature but below the melting point of the resin. Monoaxial orientation is very simple and can be done on film made by any of the standard processes, except that if blown film is used, it must first be slit and separated into single films. Film is run over a set of driven pull rollers, which are generally heated to the desired orienting temperature. It may then be passed through an oven or liquid bath to maintain orienting temperature, and is then run over another set of pull rolls running at a higher speed. Depending on the effect desired the second set may run 2-10 times as fast as the first. Monoaxially oriented film is very strong in the direction of stretching, but very weak at right angles. To obtain strengthening in both directions, the film must be stretched crossways after being stretched lengthwise.

Cross orientation is done in a tenter frame, which consists of two continuous chains which carry clips to grasp the edges of the film. The chains run on two tracks that move wider apart as they go along, thus stretching the film sideways. The assembly is housed in an oven to control temperature. A tenter frame is expensive, and because of the complicated mechanical linkages it is limited in speed. Many other devices have been tried for this purpose, but they have only had very limited success.

Shrinkable Film

Polyolefin film can be made so that when heated up to a certain temperature it will shrink. The best shrink film is made by cross-linking followed by orientation. This process is limited to low density polyethylene, since cross-linking of other polyolefins is not yet a commercial process. To cross-link film it is subjected to intense electromagnetic radiation. This is generally done by means of an electron gun, although it has been done experimentally by nuclear radiation. This radiation develops a network structure in the polymer which does not break up by heating. The cross-linked film is then heated, stretched in one or both directions just to the extent of the desired shrinkage, and is then cooled. When this film is heated, it will shrink back to its size at the time of irradiation.

A film with less precise shrink properties can be made by the blown film process, using low extrusion temperatures and high blow-up ratios. This results in a certain degree of orientation which will be released on heating, but it is not as readily controlled as the cross-linked type.

Oriented tapes

Narrow tapes useful for weaving into coarse heavy duty fabrics are made by slitting film into narrow tapes and then giving them a high degree of linear stretch at a suitable orienting temperature. Similar tapes can be made from highly monoaxially oriented film, slit after orienting. At very high orientation the crosswise strength of the tape becomes so low that it can be fibrillated into a mass of fine fibers, giving a strand similar to a coarse textile fiber. This is done mainly with linear polyethylene and polypropylene. It is much more common outside the United States.

EXTRUDED HEAVY SHEETING

Sheeting from 30-250 mils thick is made on equipment somewhat like that used for chill cast film. The die openings are, of course, wider, and this makes impractical the control of thickness by changing the die opening only. Sheeting dies therefore have a variable restriction in the slot between the manifold and the die lips, which may be moved to obtain uniform flow across the die. This is called a choker bar. The die lips themselves are usually set at a constant opening near the desired sheet thickness. Instead of the single chill roll, sheeting is usually taken from the die to a vertical stack of three or five temperature controlled polished rolls. The hot sheet from the die goes either between the two top or the two bottom rolls. The distance between these rolls is adjusted to exactly that required to produce the desired sheet thickness. This is, of course, slightly wider than sheet thickness because there is shrinkage on cooling. Roll and extruder speeds are adjusted so that the sheet contacts both rolls, but without accumulating a "bank" of excess material that cannot pass through the nip. In this way both sides of the sheet get a polished surface from contact with the rolls, and variations in sheet thickness are ironed out by the rolls. Excess material will cause a rough or rippled surface on the sheet.

The sheet is then led down the stack or up, depending on whether it was introduced at the top or bottom, passing between the second roll and the third, and around the third, as shown in Figure 5.18.

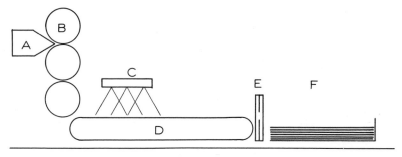

Figure 5.18. Sheet production equipment. A. Extrusion die. B. Roll stack. C. Water spray. D. Conveyor. E. Cutter. F. Stacker.

If there are five rolls it makes a similar "S" pass over these. The nips after the initial one generally are not closed enough to put appreciable pressure on the sheet. The rolls in the stack are generally at a temperature below the melting point of the polymer, but not cold enough to stiffen the sheet too much because, especially on heavy sheet, it must be kept warm enough to follow the rolls without buckling. When the sheet leaves the stack it is set up but still warm, and is carried along a roller conveyor where it is cooled by air jets, or, in some cases, by water spray. When fully cool it may be rolled up if flexible enough, or cut into sheets and stacked if it is too stiff to roll. All polyolefins may be made into sheet in this way.

INJECTION MOLDING

Injection molding is a very versatile process for making a wide variety of objects from polyolefins. It is so widely used for thermoplastics of all sorts that it will not be described in the same detail as other methods more typical of polyolefins, but large tonnages of polyolefins are processed in this way.

In this process molten plastic is forced under high pressure, which may be 10,000 psi or even more, into a closed, chilled mold. The mold remains closed until the part has solidified, then the mold is opened. Ejection mechanisms in the mold then force the part out of the mold, and the mold recloses to receive another charge. It was formerly common to have molds without automatic ejection, and the operator had to remove the part from the mold by hand. This is still done with some very large pieces, but almost all modern molds have automatic ejection of parts.

Clamp Sections

There are two main parts to an injection molding machine, the injection section and the clamp mechanism. While there are many kinds of clamp mechanisms, most modern machines have one of two kinds, toggle or hydraulic. In a hydraulic clamp a large hydraulic cylinder holds the mold closed during filling and pulls it open by retracting. This method is used mostly on very large machines or machines on which many mold changes are made, because adjustment to molds of different sizes is easier on such machines. Toggle clamps are more commonly used because the mechanical advantage of the toggle permits clamping force to be produced by a much smaller hydraulic cylinder and requires less pumping capacity. Two general types of toggle are used: the mono toggle and the double toggle. Figure 5.19 shows the two types.

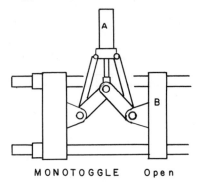

MONOTOGGLE   Open   Figure. 5.19. Two types of toggle clamp.

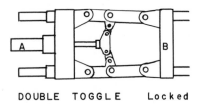

DOUBLE TOGGLE   Locked

A toggle consists of a rod, hinged in the center, joined to the mold at one end and to the frame at the other. A hydraulic cylinder straightens the rod to clamp the mold. In the closed position the toggle is essentially a straight rod between the mold and frame. In order to function properly, very exact adjustment is essential. To open the mold the cylinder pushes the center of the rod to one side of the line between mold and frame, causing it to fold up and open the mold.

Injection Sections

The injection section receives and melts the resin, and forces it into the mold.

As with most polyolefin processing methods, the resin is melted and moved to the die by means of a screw extruder. The continuous flow of the extruder in this case must be changed into an intermittent flow to fill the mold. Two methods are used to accomplish this, the reciprocating screw and the accumulator method. In the reciprocating screw machine the screw, in addition to rotating, can also move back and forth along its axis. The screw rotates, while a valve at the front of the cylinder is closed. The pressure of the melt accumulating in front of the screw forces it backwards against a light pressure. When the backwards movement of the screw reaches a preset point, which indicates that enough melt is ready to fill the mold, screw rotation stops. When the mold is closed and ready for a charge, the valve is opened, and the screw is moved forward under high hydraulic pressure and injects the melt into the mold.

In the accumulator method the screw rotation fills a cylinder with melt, against a lightly loaded plunger. When the plunger is back far enough to indicate that enough molten material is available, screw rotation stops. When the mold is ready to receive a charge, a valve which allowed passage of melt from the screw to the cylinder is shifted to connect the cylinder to the nozzle which goes into the mold. The plunger then moves forward under high hydraulic pressure and injects the plastic into the mold. Originally injection molding machines had no screw, a plunger simply pushed resin through a heating cylinder where it melted by conduction, and then was forced into a mold. Machines of this sort are still in operation, but except for some special purposes they are obsolescent.

A recently developed method melts the resin by passing it between a rotating cone and a closely spaced stationary one, and then to an injection cylinder. This is said to have an advantage in that only a small amount of material is heated at a time, so that the melt is at the high temperature for a shorter time and suffers less degradation. These machines have not been in service long enough for an assessment of their competitive advantages to be made.

High injection speed is very important for polyolefin service. This is particularly true with linear polyethylene and polypropylene. If injection speed is too slow, the melt cools before it reaches the farthest parts of the mold, resulting in internal stresses that cause warpage and cracking in the finished part.

Injection Molds

Using the proper mold is essential to good operation. Except for very large pieces it is advantageous to make a number of pieces at one shot. These may all be different. When the different pieces all enter into a single assembly, it is convenient to make them all at once. But in most polyolefin applications a number of identical pieces will be made at one time. To make a number of pieces the mold must have a series of channels connecting the main injection point to the individual cavities. This is called the runner system. Formerly runner systems were cooled and ejected with the finished part. This required cutting the parts from the runner, regrinding the runners, and returning them to the system. This was an added operation, and the remelting deteriorated resin quality. This method also reduced the useful production of the machine, because resin for all the useless runner system had to be injected into the mold each time. This has led to the development of "hot runner" or "insulated runner" systems. In a hot runner system the channels are in a separate plate which is kept hot. It is difficult to keep it hot because it needs to be so close to the cold mold. Actual contact can be avoided, except in the small areas around each passage where melt passes from the runner plate to the mold, but even this small contact area causes trouble both by heating the mold, and by cooling the runners and causing melt to freeze. This has led to insulated runner systems, where the runners are in a separate plate but this plate is not heated. The runners are protected from freezing up simply by being much thicker than the part being molded. This means that, while a layer of material freezes up around the outside of the runner, the interior remains hot and molten between shots. The low thermal conductivity of polyolefins makes this possible. It is, of course, necessary to have the runner system in a split plate, which can be readily opened up if the runners do freeze up because of some interruption of the molding process. The runner plate generally is located between the molds and the injection section, but some molds are made with a runner plate between two molds back to back, which doubles the number of parts that can be made at one time. These are called "stack" or "sandwich" molds. They are only useful for small, very high production items, where the extreme complexity and high cost of the molds can be justified by volume production. In these molds a melt channel must be provided through the center of the mold nearest the injection section.

Injection molds are generally chrome plated and highly polished because the piece takes on the mold finish. However, parts have a great tendency to stick in highly polished molds, so that it is preferable, whenever the nature of the product makes it possible, to have the mold surface slightly roughened. A very fine sand blasting may make very little difference in the appearance of the piece, and still make it much easier to remove the part from the mold.

It is also very important that the molds used in polyolefin service be maintained at a uniform temperature, because temperature variations also cause warpage and cracking.

Mold Gating

The gate is the opening whereby the plastic enters the mold. This inevitably produces a defect in the part surface, and there are many ingenious methods for minimizing this defect. In a small part the gate can be made very small. This is called pinpoint gating. If this small gate is placed in an inconspicuous place it may do no harm. Another form of restricted gate is the fan gate; here the entrance to the mold is wide but very thin, coming in at the edge of the part where it is not noticeable. Cylindrical parts may be ring gated; in this case the gate goes all around the edge of the part and is very thin. In large parts, of course, it is necessary to have a large gate to get rapid filling of the mold, and all that can be done is to locate it where it is inconspicuous.

Automatic removal of the parts from the mold is accomplished by moveable pins, rings, and other devices which are automatically actuated as the mold opens, either by the motion of the mold itself or by auxilliary hydraulic cylinders. These push the part out of the mold, and then resume their retracted position when the mold closes again. Compressed air may be used in conjunction with the mechanical means.

BLOW MOLDING

While the blowing of plastic bottles was practiced before the polyolefins were discovered, this process is now mainly associated with polyolefins. It is the process using the largest volume of linear polyethylene, and more than half of the production of linear polyethylene is blow molded. Low-density polyethylene is also blow molded in some volume, and small amounts of other polyolefins are blow molded.

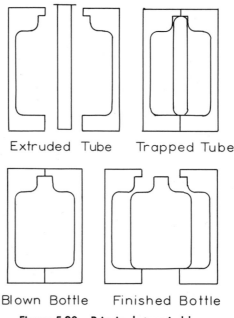

Extruded Tube   Trapped Tube

Blown Bottle   Finished Bottle

Figure 5.20. Principal steps in blow molding.

Basically blow molding is the same operation that has been used for centuries to make glass bottles. In its adaptation to plastics it consists of several steps. A tube of molten plastic is extruded downwards out of a die; this is called a parison. While the plastic is still hot, a mold in the shape of the outside of the finished part is clamped around the molten tube, closing off the bottom of the tube. Air pressure is then introduced into the inside of the tube, blowing it out until it touches the mold on all sides. After a brief cooling period the mold is opened, and the part removed. Figure 5.20 shows the steps in this process diagrammatically.

The blow molding machine consists of two sections: an extruder or parison preparation section, and the clamping and blowing section.

Extruded Parisons

Two general methods are used to adapt the continuous flow of the extruder to the intermittent need for a parison. The most common is to use two or more dies with a valving system that diverts the flow to another die when a parison has been completed. It is also possible to use molds that move away from the die as soon as they have closed on the parison, allowing continuous parison formation to take place at a single die. In both of these methods the extruder runs continuously. For very large pieces, where extruding at the extruder output rate would be too slow, the accumulator method is used. In this method the extruder pumps melt into a cylinder in front of a plunger. When a sufficient supply of melt has been produced, a valve connects the cylinder to the die, and the entire contents of the cylinder is extruded rapidly through the die. The extruder screw is usually, but not necessarily stopped during this process.

Molded Parisons

A parison may also be produced by injection molding. In this process a mold the shape of the outside of the desired parison is made; a hollow, porous mandrel is placed in the mold to form the inside of the parison. Melt is injected into the mold and, before it has a chance to cool, the mold is opened and the parison is taken out of the mold on the mandrel. Parison and mandrel are then placed in the blowing mold, and air is blown into the mandrel, separating the parison from it and conforming it to the mold. This method allows very accurate parison formation, which means good control of bottle wall thickness.

Clamping Mechanisms   The clamping mechanism on blow molding machines varies a great deal. The pressure inside a blow mold is only that of the blowing air, and this is generally under 60 psi. This means that blow molds do not have to be very heavily constructed, and do not require heavy clamping mechanisms. The design freedom resulting from these moderate clamping requirements makes it possible to vary the clamping mechanism to accomplish other purposes. Multiple die machines generally have very simple clamps which open and close the mold by means of air cylinders. Single die machines, however, have relatively complicated clamp mechanisms which not only open and close the mold, but also move the mold away from the vicinity of the die after clamping. Such machines may use from two to eight or more molds. Two mold machines simply move the two molds alternately under the die and away from it. The multiple mold units index the molds under the die, and away either on a horizontal plane, called carrosel, or in a vertical plane, called ferris wheel. In the ferris wheel method the parison is not necessarily cut each time, but the speed of mold movement may be adapted to the extrusion rate, so that one mold after the other simply clamps onto the continuously forming parison.

Parison Shape Control

Originally a straight cylindrical parison was used, but when this is blown to the shape of the bottle it produces a bottle of uneven thickness. This is particularly true if the bottle is not round. This problem was the original incentive for going to the injection molded parison, because such a parison could be made with variations in thickness corresponding to the requirements of the particular object being blown, and give a molding with even walls. At the present time it is possible to vary the shape of extruded parisons almost as readily as can be done by molding. To compensate for noncylindrical bottle shapes, the extrusion die shape is changed to give a thicker parison wall opposite those places where the bottle is widest, this providing more material where it must stretch the farthest. The extrusion die is also provided with a moveable mandrel which can change wall thickness along the length of the parison to provide extra material to reinforce the bottom or shoulders of a bottle, for instance. These techniques allow the blow molder to use material economically by putting more plastic in critical places without increasing over-all weight very much.

The blow molding process is used mainly for making bottles, but it also is a very good method for making a wide variety of hollow articles that are not in any sense bottles. It is widely used for toys and is very good for large sized thin walled articles such as garbage cans, where can and top can be molded as a single unit and cut apart for use.

Blow molding has a special advantage which makes it the preferred method of producing some articles that could readily be made by injection molding. Blow molding does not require as good flow properties as injection molding, therefore polyolefins of higher molecular weight can be used for blow molding. These higher molecular weight resins have superior physical properties, so a part will be stronger if made the same weight, or can have the same strength with less material.

EXTRUSION COATING AND LAMINATING

Polyolefins are very widely used as extrusion coating and laminating materials. We are distinguishing between coating and laminating by considering a coating as a layer of polyolefin placed over the surface of another material, while laminating with a polyolefin melt consists of placing the polyolefin between two layers of other materials.

Polyolefin extrusion coatings are widely used on paper and paperboard as a means of waterproofing, and are also used on aluminum foil, cellophane, and other materials as a convenient heat seal medium.

Extrusion Coating Equipment

The equipment used for extrusion coating closely resembles that used in the chill roll casting method of making film. Addition of a letoff mechanism for the substrate used, a pressure roll to press substrate and coating to the chill roll, and some slight modification of the die, are all that is different. Figure 5.21 is a diagram of the equipment.

Substrate treatment or priming stations are commonly found on extrusion coating machines. These treat the substrate in order to improve adhesion of the coating or other coating properties. There are many kinds of these, only a few of which will be mentioned. Flame treating of Kraft paper, practiced mainly to burn off protruding fibers, which might penetrate the coating, consists simply of playing a gas flame against the surface of the substrate. Corona treating of glossy substrates is identical to the corona treatment of polyolefin film for printing. It is used to improve coating adhesion. Priming is practiced to improve adhesion of the coating. This designates the

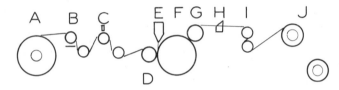

Figure 5.21. Polyolefin extrusion coating. A. Substrate let-off roll. B. Tension control. C. Treater or primer. D. Pressure roll. E. Extrusion die. F. Chill roll. G. Stripper roll. H. Trimmer. I. Pull roll. J. Winder.

application of some liquid, usually with some residue on evaporation, to the substrate. A priming station generally also includes a drier to remove the liquid. Water is used as primer on some paper stocks, and promotes adhesion simply by roughening the paper surface a little. Resin emulsions are commonly used; these may contain styrene copolymers, polyvinylidene chloride, or other polymers. In the case of polyvinylidene chloride the primer not only promotes adhesion but also adds to the barrier properties of the structure. Organic solvent solutions of titanium esters are also used. In this case the priming station includes a drier to remove the solvent, followed by a steam chest to hydrolize the ester.

Extrusion coating requires very high melt temperatures in order to get good adhesion to the substrate in the absence of an effective primer. Therefore the extruders used to prepare the melt are longer than those used for other purposes, often having an L/D ratio above $30/1$. The screws used in these machines are also unique in having very long metering zones, often more than half the length of the screw, and these metering zones are shallow for the size of the screw. These extruder characteristics are needed because the high temperatures required cannot be achieved simply by frictional heating. When a polyolefin melt gets very hot its viscosity is so low that the shear developed by screw rotation is no longer high enough to produce much heat. The extruder must therefore have a lot of surface area to expose the melt to heat conduction to reach the high temperatures.

The extrusion coating die differs from the chill roll cast film die in that the shape of the face of the die may be modified in such a way as to allow the die lips to reach down close to the nip between the chill roll and pressure roll. This is to prevent excessive cooling of the melt before it comes in contact with the substrate.

Coating dies also commonly have a feature rarely used on film dies. This is some device for adjusting the die width, commonly called deckels. These may be rods placed inside the die lips, but are more commonly external covers over the die lip opening. The deckels are used to adjust the coating width to the substrate width, which is very important to avoid waste of material. In some cases the coating is made a little narrower than the substrate, and the coated material is then trimmed to remove the bare substrate. Since substrates are generally more expensive than the polyolefin coating, it is much more common to "overcoat", which means to make a coating wider than the substrate, and trim the excess coating.

The pressure roll has a resilient coating so that it can press against the chill roll without damaging it. Neoprene or silicone rubber are often used as roll facings, and there may also be a thin layer of "Teflon" * tape over this, especially at the ends of the roll to prevent sticking of the melt overcoating.

While the chill roll used for film casting is almost always highly polished, other finishes are often used on coating lines. This is done for several reasons, the most important being to control the frictional qualities of the coating. Many coated substrates are converted, that is made into end use products on high speed machinery that requires the coating to slip over metal guides or, in some cases, against itself. Highly polished coating surfaces tend to stick or at least not slip reliably in these circumstances. A slight roughening of the surface

* Trademark of duPont.

can greatly improve slip properties. If a glossy appearance is needed but with improved slip, a special roll finish called "mirror pocket" is used. As its name implies this finish contains minute depressions that are highly polished inside. The coating pressed against it therefore has very small shiny raised areas, which help it slip, but give the coating a glossy appearance. In many cases, of course, gloss is not needed, so various sand blasted or matte finishes are used. For decorative effects textured or embossed rolls are available.

The rest of the equipment is generally like that used for flat film. Trim scrap generated in coating operations can rarely be reused because of contamination with the substrate, so it is generally burned.

When the polyolefin melt is to be used as an adhesive between two other materials, a letoff for the second substrate must be provided above the chill roll, which is arranged so that it may feed the substrate in over the top of the chill roll. The other substrate comes in over the pressure roll in the normal manner for coating, and the olefin melt goes between the two substrates where they come together at the intersection of the chill roll and pressure roll. A lamination completely adhered across the whole width can be made in this way, but in some cases it is desired to have adhesion only in certain areas, leaving other parts free. This can readily be done by modifying the die to give bands of melt where the adhesion is needed, and leaving the rest of the width free. A similar effect can be obtained by a pressure roll modified to press only certain areas. This permits a continuous olefin coating but only partial adhesion.

Coextruded Laminations

Composite films consisting of two or three layers of different polyolefins are often made by coextrusion. This is done on chill roll cast or waterbath film equipment, but the product is more nearly related to the present subject, so it will be discussed here. In this process two extruders are used to feed a single die. The two melts are introduced into opposite sides of the die for a two layer construction, and flow through the die passages and the die lips together. Rather astonishingly, there is no appreciable mixing of the two melts as they flow through the die. This is because flow in plastic melts is entirely laminar, due to their high viscosity. The melts then emerge from the die lips as a single firmly bonded film. The relative thickness of the two layers is determined by the relative speed of the two extruders. Quality control of relative thickness depends on finding some composite property to check, because the two layers are so firmly bound that they cannot be separated. In the popular low density polyethylene-polypropylene laminates, for instance, yield strength is a function of the relative amounts of the resins and can be used for quality control. The difference in certain infrared absorption bands may be used for the same purpose, and this has the advantage of being adaptable to continuous on-line monitoring.

Three layer constructions can be made in the same way with one melt coming in between the other two. Some care must be taken in the configuration of die passages to assure that three even layers start into the die, but once they are established they flow quite uniformly through the die. In experimental work this can be established readily by coloring the layers different colors.

It is necessary to select the grades of resin used, so that at the temperature and flow rate of the equipment, they have similar flow resistance; otherwise, flow instability may appear and disrupt the layers.

The Use of Masterbatch

Polyolefin coatings are frequently pigmented for appearance or for resistance to ultraviolet light damage. Precolored resins may be used for this purpose, but generally a color concentrate or *masterbatch*, which contains the desired pigment in high concentration in a polyolefin base, is added to the regular coating resin. If the masterbatch is made with a suitable base resin, and has good dispersion of the pigment, then the resulting coating will be as uniformly colored as one made from precolored resin.

Masterbatch is also used to introduce additives other than colors. For instance, it is often necessary to control the coefficient of friction of a coating by the addition of slip additives to the resin. These same additives may also be used to prevent sticking of the coating to the chill roll, where this is a problem. These additives may be obtained in masterbatch form and added to the resin as needed. Other sorts of additives like antioxidants, ultraviolet stabilizers, antistatic agents, and others, may also be added to the resin in masterbatch form.

The use of masterbatch with a single base resin greatly reduces the inventory problems when a wide variety of different coating formulations is used in the plant.

POLYOLEFIN PIPE PRODUCTION

Polyethylene is the most widely used polyolefin for plastic pipe. Both low density and linear polyethylene, and mixtures of the two are used. Polybutene-1 has limited use, especially in conjunction with linear polyethylene and polypropylene. Pipe is made from very high molecular weight linear polyethylene by proprietary methods. Cross-linked polyethylene pipe, and biaxially oriented polypropylene pipe have been described, but have not yet obtained appreciable commercial usage.

The methods used for the largest volume production of low density polyethylene, and low density-linear blends will be described.

The most common pipe die design is similar to that shown in Figure 5.22.

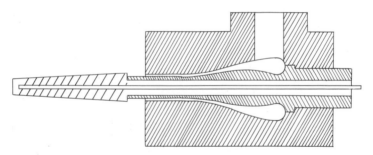

Figure 5.22. A pipe extrusion die with an extended mandrel.

A die of this kind may be mounted across the front of an extruder, or it may be mounted with a right angle connection to the extruder, so that the pipe is formed parallel to the extruder, in which case it is called an offset die. Dies are usually designed with interchangeable cores and bushings, so that several pipe sizes may be made from the same basic die. The extended mandrel shown is optional.

The basic problem in pipe extrusion is supporting and maintaining the shape and dimensions of the pipe just after it leaves the die and is still hot and soft. The main variations in pipe lines occur at this point. The extended mandrel shown is one common device for this purpose. The mandrel is water cooled, and in use water is generally flowed over the outside of the hot pipe while it is passing over the mandrel. If the system is operating properly the pipe will be self-supporting when it leaves the end of the mandrel, and it may be further cooled by water spray or immersion in a water bath. The other most generally used method is the external vacuum sizing die. In this method a cylindrical die with internal dimensions the size of the outside of the desired pipe is equipped with small holes in an area a little in from one end, and a vacuum is drawn on these holes. The hot pipe is led into the die, and the vacuum holds the surface of the pipe against the inside of the sizing die. The surface between pipe and sizing die is generally water lubricated, and the sizing die itself is water cooled. Here again the pipe should be self-supporting when it leaves the die. Sometimes a combination of these two methods is used; the pipe comes from the end of the extended mandrel still warm and is led to the sizing die. This combination permits higher extrusion rates than either alone. There are also other methods but these are in less use.

Whatever the initial cooling method, final cooling is generally done by immersion in a long water tank, after which the pipe goes to the capstan which determines the line speed, and is either rolled up or cut into lengths depending on its size and stiffness.

Polyolefin Monofilament

This book has been limited to the plastic uses of polyolefins, but in some cases it is difficult to draw the line between plastics and textiles. Monofilament is essentially the same thing as textile fiber except larger in diameter, and it finds application in many traditional textile uses like fishing line, furniture webbing, sewing thread, twine, marine cordage. However, the main monofilament manufacturers have been separate from strictly textile fiber manufacturers, and the equipment for monofilament production, while hybrid in nature, has tended towards the traditional plastics machinery. For this reason it will be treated very briefly here.

Monofilament is generally extruded through a conventional screw extruder of rather small size, $2\frac{1}{2}$ inch diameter being typical. The die consists of a series of small holes which may be arranged in a line, but more commonly in a circular pattern of several rows, because in this way more orifices may be placed in a small area. The holes are about three times the diameter of the desired monofilament size, and a die may have 60-80 holes. Pump type dies like those used in fiber extrusion may also be used for monofilament. In these dies a small positive displacement pump is located within the die and assures a uniform flow of polymer, regardless of pressure fluctuations from the extruder.

The monofilaments are extruded downwards into a water tank and then go in a group to a set of pull rolls. These are called *godets* in this industry. This first set of godets determines the rate of draw from the die and also the strand diameter. From the first godets the filaments go to an oven or a tank of hot liquid which is at the proper drawing temperature, and then to another set of godets which run more rapidly than the first. Typically the second set will go at 9-12 times the speed of the first. This draws the fiber to develop the tensile strength and also brings it to the final diameter.

From the second godets there may be another oven and another set of godets running slightly slower, to set the monofilament and reduce shrinkage. After the last godets the filaments are separated, and each one is wound on a separate spool.

The physical properties of the filament depend on the degree of stretching and the temperature of stretching. Polypropylene and linear polyethylene typically draw at 350-400°F, while low density polyethylene may be drawn at 200-300°F.

PROCESSING POWDERED POLYOLEFINS

There are several processing methods that start with finely powdered resin. Low density polyethylene is the most commonly used, although some linear is used in this way.

Rotational Molding

This is the most widely used powder processing method. A light weight split mold is used. A charge of powdered resin which is the weight desired in the finished piece is placed into the open mold, and the mold is clamped together. The closed mold is placed into a rotator, which turns it on two axes, so that powder tumbles evenly over all inside surfaces of the mold. The mold and rotator are placed in an oven which heats the mold until the polymer is melted and coated evenly over the inside of the mold. The mold is cooled then by air or a water spray and opened to remove the part. This process produces a hollow part without any opening, and can make parts of very uniform wall thickness. Molding cycles are rather long so a large number of molds is required for any considerable production. The process is not used for very large production items but is used for toys and some industrial items.

Powder Coating

Rugs are sometimes backed with polyolefins by spreading a layer of powder on the back of the rug and melting the polymer by radiant heat. Rugs backed in this way may be heat formed and will retain their contours, which is convenient for processes like automotive carpeting.

Metal parts may be powder coated by heating the part above the polymer melting point, and dipping it into a fluidized bed of polymer powder. Powder will stick to the metal and coat it. A reheating is usually used to smooth and polish the coating. Additional layers of coating may be added by reheating and redipping, but this deteriorates the first polymer layer, so is rarely advisable.

Powder may be applied to large metal areas by flame spraying. In this method a flame gun is used which can blow plastic powder through the center of the flame. The flame is used to preheat the metal part to the polymer melting point, powder is then blown through the flame, where it melts and sticks to the metal when it hits it. In this process generally a base layer of a rubbery polymer is put down first, followed by the polyolefin.

FOAMED POLYOLEFINS

Polyolefin foams are used as resilient gasketing materials, and as light weight insulation. Two general foaming methods are used, direct foaming by the addition of gas or a volatile liquid, and the use of a foaming agent which is solid when added but decomposes to release a gas when heated to final processing temperature.

The direct addition of gas is usually done in an extruder. The extruder barrel is equipped with inlets for gas near the front where the plastic mass is molten and under pressure. High pressure gas, usually nitrogen, is blown into the melt, but the pressure is high enough so that there is little expansion of the gas. The extruder screw, opposite the entry points, is modified to promote good mixing between polymer and gas. The mixed mass is then extruded through a die, and expands from the pressure drop. While simple in principle this is difficult to practice and many ingenious devices have been invented to make it possible. This method can make a very low density foam and is usually made in sheet form to use as gasketing.

Volatile hydrocarbons can also be used in an extruder for the same purpose; however, it is possible to use these simply by saturating the extruder feed with the volatile material.

Solid foaming agents are generally compounds that release nitrogen on heating. Azodicarbonamide, which is sold under several trade names, is most comonly used for low density polyethylene. Linear polyethylene and polypropylene require a material of higher decomposition temperature, and these are also available commercially. The foaming agent is first well dispersed in the resin at a temperature below its decomposition temperature, and is then extruded into final form, above the decomposition temperature of the foaming agent. Foamed polyethylene is used for wire coating. Azodicarbonamide and some other foaming agents have an added advantage that in addition to producing nitrogen they are also free radical sources, so that they cross-link the resin to some extent while foaming it, thereby increasing its abrasion resistance and softening point.

Foamed polyolefins may be injection molded as well as extruded. In this process the melt containing a foaming agent is kept under enough pressure to prevent expansion until the time of injection. Only enough melt to fill part of the mold is injected, and the expansion fills the mold. The material which contacts the mold walls is cooled so quickly that it does not expand much, resulting in a part with a solid skin and a foamed core.

POLYOLEFIN WIRE AND CABLE COATING

Wire insulation was one of the first uses of polyethylene and is still an important polyolefin market. The resin most commonly used is low density polyethylene. Some linear polyethylene and a considerable amount of copolymers of both linear and low density types are used.

As with so many of these processing methods, melt is prepared in a screw extruder and forced through a die. The die in this case is essentially a tube die, but the mandrel of the die has a hole through it to allow a wire to be passed inside the polymer tube. There are two basic forms. In one form the die mandrel ends some distance before the opening of the die, so that the wire itself acts as mandrel during the passage through the die lips. This type of die is used for large wire and particularly for cable covering, because it allows plastic to be forced into the outer windings of the cable, thus anchoring the coating and reinforcing the construction mechanically. In the other version the die mandrel extends to the die lips, so that a tube slightly larger than the wire is produced, and then is drawn down into good contact with the wire by the stretching caused by the haul-off speed. In both types of die, a vacuum may be drawn around the wire to assure the absence of air bubbles at the plastic-wire interface.

The wire line consists of a wire let-off which should have good automatic tension control, a wire straightener to assure the absence of kinks or bends, and a wire heater. It is necessary to heat the wire in order to obtain good adhesion of plastic to metal, and to preclude air containing separations which could produce internal corona discharge in service, which rapidly destroys the wire. The most common wire preheater provides for two metal contact rollers with some length of wire between them. A low voltage, high amperage current is passed through the wire between the rollers, raising its temperature. Oven preheat may also be used, but this takes much more space.

From the preheater the wire goes directly through the die, where it is covered with plastic, and from there into a water tank for cooling. Thin coverings are generally plunged directly into cold water, but heavy ones may be air cooled for a distance first, and may also be immersed first into warm water, because sudden chilling of heavy walls may produce voids.

The cooled wire is then run over capstan rolls, which determine the speed of the wire, and from there to a reel. The reel mechanism should have a good tension control to assure a uniformly wound reel.

CROSS-LINKED POLYETHYLENE

In order to improve the strength, abrasion resistance, and heat resistance of low density polyethylene wire insulation, it is cross-linked. This is done by using a compound containing a peroxide cross-linking agent, extruding it at a temperature below the decomposition point of the peroxide, and passing the coated wire through a vulcanization tube after it leaves the die.

A continuous vulcanization (CV) tube consists of a steel tube, which may be a hundred feet or more in length and is covered with thermal insulation. At each end of the tube there is a pressure lock which permits the insulated wire to go through, but allows a build-up of pressure within the tube. High pressure steam is admitted into the tube to raise the temperature to a level above the point where the cross-linking agent becomes active.

CV tubes may be either straight or catenary in form. Since the insulation is soft and readily deformed during most of its path through the tube, it cannot be allowed to touch the tube or to be supported in any way while in the tube. This means that the wire must be supported before it enters and after it leaves the tube. Since electrical conductor wire, whether copper or aluminum, cannot withstand very great tension, the wire sags considerably while passing through the tube.

This means that a long tube must have a fairly large diameter to permit the sag without wall contact. For this reason many very long CV tubes are built in catenary shape, which follows the sag of the wire, and which functions just as well with a smaller diameter tube. In this tube the coating is heated above the decomposition temperature of the peroxide, and the polyethylene is cross-linked. It is then cooled and reeled up as before.

This process has broadened the uses of polyethylene insulated wire to include power applications, where it had previously been excluded because of its low softening temperature.

FABRICATION AND CONVERSION

Many of the processing methods that have been described produce articles that are ready for an end use; some of them, however, produce an intermediate product that requires further operations before it is useful. These operations are called fabricating and converting. The products concerned are film and sheeting, and to a limited extent rods and tubes.

Thermoforming

Polyethylene sheeting is very often made into a finished product by thermoforming. This process consists of heating a sheet of polyolefin, usually clamped in a frame, until it has softened enough to stretch very readily, and then forcing the plastic web into conformity with a mold by suction, pressure, mechanical action, or a combination of these forces.

Thermoforming is, at this point, such a complicated family of techniques that we cannot do more than suggest some of the methods used.

The film is usually heated by means of high intensity infrared heating elements, usually one on each side of the sheet. These are called *sandwich* heaters. Ovens, hot gas jets, or contact with heated surfaces may also be used.

Heavy sheeting is usually handled by the sheet, with a frame indexing between the heating and forming station, carrying the sheet. Thin sheeting is handled in rolls, with only the edges of the web being clamped; passage through the oven and molding stations may be continuous or intermittent. In intermittent motion, a length of sheet will first be held in the heating station for the needed time, and then the heated portion will be moved to the molding station, bringing a new length between the heaters. Continuous operation may be obtained by using moving molds that synchronize their motion with that of the sheet. The molds may be carried on chain conveyors or on a rotating drum. There is no standard nomenclature for the forming methods but the following paragraphs describe a few of them.

Vacuum Forming   In this method the heated sheet is positioned over a female mold, and the edges sealed to the mold. Vacuum is then drawn in the mold to pull the plastic into conformity with the mold. Simple vacuum forming is limited to fairly shallow draws, otherwise the bottom of the molded piece thins out excessively. If deeper parts are needed, a mechanical plunger is used to push the softened web down into the mold. This is called "plug assist". The plug is always smaller than the mold, but may be shaped like it, just leaving a small clearance all around, or sometimes the plug only goes in part way. In either case vacuum is drawn to pull the plastic from the plug and form it to the mold. The plug may also be perforated so that air pressure can assist this process.

Drape Forming This is essentially vacuum forming on male molds. The soft sheet is drawn down over the male mold and sealed to the mold base. Vacuum is then drawn through holes in the low spots of the mold to conform the sheet closely to the mold. If a container is made in this way, the bottom will be thicker than the top, because the hot sheet first contacts the bottom of the mold where it is slightly cooled, before the stretching down the sides is completed. One of the main problems with this method, particularly when multiple molds are used, is called "webbing". Webbing occurs because when the hot sheet is drawn down over an angle in the mold, it tends to fold and stick together rather than remain a single sheet. One of the ways in which this is remedied is to use a drape assist, which presses the plastic to the mold base around each individual mold.

Pressure Forming This may be done with either male or female molds, and differs only in that positive pressure is applied to the sheet instead of, or in addition to vacuum on the mold. The advantage is that much greater pressures are possible, making it useful for thicker sheet, and making it possible to form at lower temperatures where the sheet is not so soft.

Matched Mold Forming In this process the soft sheet is trapped between a male and female metal mold, which are designed to leave just the space needed for the plastic. This permits the most accurate and the most rapid forming. In its final development it becomes sheet stamping, which will be described in more detail under future developments, because it is not at present used to its potential.

Film Conversion

Film conversion is also a complex of many techniques which may be classified into printing or decorating on the one hand and joining or sealing on the other. The principle end uses are packages.

Printing Polyolefin film is printed in four different ways. By far the most common is the flexographic process. The printing plate in this method is made of flexible rubber or plastic and is supported on a metal roller. An inking roller applies ink to the plate, and the film runs between the plate and a backing roller, picking up ink in the process. The low cost and easy interchangeability of the printing plates makes this particularly suitable for printing bags or other packages where relatively frequent change of plates is necessary. This does not produce the highest quality of printing, but the process has undergone a great deal of development and produces printing that is quite acceptable for most packaging applications, and that may be done at relatively high speeds. It is not unusual to print in line with a film extrusion operation by this method.

The best quality of printing is done by the rotogravure process, where the design is etched into a metal roller as a series of small dots. This method can produce subtle shadings and very fine detail at very high speeds. It is suitable for long runs of the same design, but the rollers are large and expensive, so that a large number of designs requires a high expenditure and much storage area. It is sometimes used for the main decorative part of package printing, where the design is identical for many packages, leaving only a small part to be done flexographically to identify a particular item.

Offset printing, where the ink is transferred from a printing plate to a rubber roller, and from that to the plastic is less frequently used for film, although it is used increasingly for items like bottle labeling.

Silk screen printing, where ink is forced through holes in a fine screen partially blocked to form the design, is used where a heavy coating of ink is needed. It is not very widely used on film, but is the most common method of printing on bottles and other relatively heavy plastic objects.

Sealing and Joining   By far the most common method of sealing polyolefin films is heat sealing. This has a variety of forms, the oldest and still common form being the hot bar sealer. In this form the two layers of film to be sealed are placed on top of each other between a heated metal bar and a flexible support. The bar is brought down on the films long enough to heat them to the point where they fuse together under pressure of the bar. The bar is then lifted and the sealed films removed. A variation of this is in the impulse sealer, where the heated bar is replaced by an unheated or even cooled bar faced by a resistance wire or tape. As before, the assembly to be sealed is clamped between the bar and a flexible support. Then a short surge of electrical current is passed through the resistance wire, heating it enough to soften the plastic. The assembly then remains clamped until the seal cools somewhat. This method is preferable for heavy film or for oriented film where the hot bar method will cause distortion of the seal. In both these methods a "Teflon" * coated glass fiber tape is usually interposed between the material being sealed and the sealing bar, to prevent sticking of the plastic to the sealing bar.

Band sealers consist of two metal tapes which run over pulleys in such a way as to be parallel and close together for part of their travel. The material to be sealed is caught between the two bands and carried into a heated area where it is melted while the tapes are pressed together. Then there is a cooled area to set the seal before the sealed area reaches the exit end of the sealer. This makes a continuous seal and is useful for long seals.

Hot wire sealing is used in many high speed bag making machines. In this process a wire heated to a high temperature where it will melt the plastic almost instantly is passed through the material to be sealed, cutting it and sealing the edges simultaneously. This makes two seals at the same time, one at each side of the cut. Side seal bags are made by this method simply by cutting and sealing the desired lengths from "J" and "U" tubing. Similar seals may be made by the hot knife method, where a heated knife is pressed against the film, cutting and sealing at the same time.

Flame sealing is used on heavy film or thicker wall constructions like collapsible tubes. The edges to be sealed are clamped together leaving a projecting edge. A flame or a high intensity infrared heater melts the edges, and they are clamped together by a cooled metal clamp to complete the seal.

This is by no means all of the heat sealing methods now in use, but it illustrates their variety. Bar and impulse seals are used on coated materials as well as unsupported film. In fact in some cases the principal purpose of the coating is to make this rapid method of sealing possible.

Available adhesives can make low strength seals between poly-olefin films that are satisfactory for some purposes. These are the

* Trademark of duPont.

tacky pressure sensitive adhesives. They never really become hard and make a solid joint but are adequate just for holding film together.

Rigid polyolefin molded parts are sometimes sealed together by ultrasonics. High frequency compression waves pass from a generator into one of the parts to be sealed together. The other part is supported on a rigid base. The ultrasonic waves produce fusion at the part interface without any great heat production. This means no part distortion and no delay for cooling, allowing fast production. The equipment is expensive, part design must be right for the purpose, and the process has not had wide use.

SIX

polyolefin plastic applications

PACKAGING

For quite a few years packaging has been the largest volume use for polyolefins, and it is one of the fastest growing industries. Polyolefins are used as film, as coatings, formed and molded containers and lids, tubes and bottles, and closures.

In order to give an idea of the relative importance of these uses, 1967 consumption figures in each category are given in Table 6.1 in millions of pounds.

TABLE 6.I. Polyolefins Used in Packaging (in million pounds)

| | Polyethylene | | | |
	Low Density	High Density	Polypropylene	EVA
Film and sheeting		800	61	
Coatings		307		20
Containers and lids		100		
Bottles and tubes	15	335		
Closures	16	18		
Total packaging		1,591	61	20

More than one and a half billion pounds of polyolefins, most of it polyethylene, were used in packaging. The polyethylene consumption in the first three categories of Table 6.1 is not classified according to density, but the greatest part of this by far is low density polyethylene.

Film and Sheeting

Fresh Produce   The first large scale civilian use of polyethylene film was in the packaging of fresh vegetables. The moisture resistance of the film reduces moisture loss from the vegetables, thus decreasing weight loss in shipping and keeping the produce in good condition longer. The relatively high oxygen and carbon dioxide transmission of the film permits the vegetable to continue a low level of respiration in the package which is essential to retard spoilage. For some vegetables the barrier properties of polyethylene film are too strong, so that the best storage conditions require some perforations in the bag. The use of polyethylene film for packaging produce is now so widespread that most of the vegetables on any vegetable counter will be packaged in polyethylene film.

Frozen Foods   Frozen vegetables are also very often packed in low density polyethylene bags. Low density polyethylene has a remarkable ability to remain tough and flexible even at low zero temperatures of food freezing. Ethylene-Vinyl Acetate copolymers show even better low temperature flexibility and are beginning to be used in these applications. The plastic bag quite adequately serves as the sole container for the frozen food, and a large quantity is sold for this purpose, usually in the large size economy pack. In some cases the plastic bag is used inside a carton, which serves mainly as a means of display.

Prepared frozen foods are also often wrapped in polyolefin film, sometimes in the form of multiple pouches, each of which contains a separate component of a dish or meal. This eliminates the need for a cluster of small separated containers, which are hard to package together and keep together until used.

Bakery Products   Bread and other bakery products are also mainly packaged in polyolefin plastic film. Here too, low density polyethylene is the most widely used, with some linear, mostly as blends with low density polyethylene, and some polypropylene, mostly as a component of a composite with low density polyethylene, also being used. The low density polyethylene bread bag is the largest single item in bakery products packaging, amounting to about 60% of the total and growing rapidly. Smaller amounts of low density polyethylene bags are used for other bakery products.

Polypropylene and linear polyethylene are used mainly for bread overwrap; this is really a holdover from older practices. When polyolefin film manufacturers first tried to penetrate the bread wrap market, it was being served by waxed paper and cellophane, which were applied on high speed wrapping machinery. It was, therefore, necessary to produce a film that could be used on the same wrapping machinery with a minimum of modification. The main obstacle was that the low density polyethylene film was too limp to feed properly into these machines. Thus, the market was first penetrated by films made from blends of linear and low density polyethylene, but these were not entirely successful. Polypropylene film was then introduced into this market but encountered sealing problems. The next developmental step was the production of laminates of polypropylene and low density polyethylene; these were made with polypropylene sandwiched between two low density polyethylene layers or with just one layer of each (linear polyethylene is also used in a manner similar to polypropylene). In these constructions stiffness and resistance to "burn through" on sealing were contributed by the polypropylene or linear component, while easy heat sealing and tear resistance were given by the low density polyethylene. These constructions are still used a good deal in bread wrap and operate very well in high speed overwrap machinery. However, they are losing out to the low density polyethylene bag, mainly because consumers show a decided preference for the bag as opposed to the overwrap.

The advantages of the bag over the wrapping are its ability to be opened easily and its reclosable feature. Opening a wrapped loaf was sometimes difficult, for the film might not tear where expected, spilling the bread, etc. The bag is held closed by a readily removable clip, which may be put back to reclose the bag. Once a wrapped loaf is opened, the wrapper no longer serves to keep the loaf together, while the bag remains intact and may be used to store the bread until it is gone.

As with fresh vegetables, polyethylene retards drying and keeps bread fresh longer than other packaging methods do. The polyethylene bags are very resistant to breakage, practically eliminating loss due to package failure.

Soft Goods   Soft goods packaging is another field taken over almost entirely by low density polyethylene bag packages. Soft goods encompass clothing, shirts, sweaters, sheets, and blankets. These are now commonly packaged in an ingenious bag, which is essentially self-closing when filled. This bag is made from a piece of tubing with a cross section shaped like that in Figure 6.1.

Figure 6.1. Cross section of film for making one kind of self-closing bag.

The bags are made by sealing and cutting across the tubing, making a side seal bag. To fill the bag the inner flap is pulled out, the article inserted, and then the outer flap is pulled, over the end of the article. The pressure of the contents, which must, of course, be a single compressible article, then holds the inner flap against the outer flap, making a closure. Generally a strip of pressure sensitive tape is put across the two flaps just for safety, but even without that, it is quite a secure closure.

The polyethylene bag is clear enough for the contents to be seen, flexible enough for them to be felt to some extent, tough enough to withstand rough handling, and serves to protect the contents against soiling.

Cast polypropylene film is used to a considerable extent in textile wrapping, and this use is growing rapidly. The superior clarity and sparkle are an advantage over polyethylene, and the stiffness results in a neater looking package. It is used mainly as a wrapping rather than as a bag, and polypropylene handles better on wrapping machinery.

Garment Bags   Closely related to soft goods packaging but in a separate category, is the laundry and dry cleaners' shirt and garment bag. Very thin low density polyethylene film is used for this purpose; the usual garment bag film is 0.3 mil thick. This thinness can be used because the plastic is remarkably tough, and because the application only requires a single short-time use. The extreme thinness of the film makes it very inexpensive. This is really the only application we will discuss where cost becomes a major consideration in the use of plastic film. For this application polyethylene film is the cheapest material that will do the job; in addition, it is better than paper because of its transparency, toughness, and easy handling.

As with many successful new plastic applications, garment bag production was made practical by a new way of dispensing the material. An extremely thin film bag is too limp to be handled like a paper bag. This problem was solved by producing the bags in a continuous roll, with easily torn perforations between the bags. This roll is supported on a dispenser which hangs above a hook supported from the floor. The garment on its hanger is hung from the hook, and a bag is unrolled from the roll and in the same motion drawn over the garment. When the end of the bag reaches the top of the garment, the perforations above the bag seal are torn through by a stroke of the hand, separating the bag from the roll and leaving the open end of the next bag ready for use.

Shrink Wrap   Carton overwrap is another large and growing field for polyethylene film. In this application the primary package is a rigid paperboard carton, and the polyethylene is wrapped over it to protect it from dirt and moisture, to give it gloss, and often to hold it shut. This is done by wrapping a sheet of film over it and sealing the edges together on the bottom or ends, much in the same way as other sheet wrapping materials are used. In recent years this method of wrapping has been replaced to a great extent by shrink packaging, where a special shrinkable film is used. The package is generally placed between two sheets of film, and the edges are heat sealed all around, giving a rather loose fitting wrap. This is then run through a shrink tunnel, where hot air or infrared heaters heat the film to its shrink temperature, where it then shrinks up into a neat tight fitting wrap. In this application a certain amount of polypropylene, in addition to low density polyethylene, is used. Shrink packaging is used in the overwrap field and to an increasing extent in produce wrapping, meat wrapping, and other types of wrapping.

Skin Packaging   Polyolefin film and sheeting are also used in skin packaging, where the film is softened and drawn down by vacuum to conform to the contours of the object packaged. This is widely used for consumer packaging of hardware and kitchenware items. Some of the polar copolymers and the ionomers are particularly well adapted to this application, because their toughness makes it possible to package objects with sharp corners or points, without danger of puncturing the film.

Polyolefin Coatings

Milk Cartons The use of low density polyethylene on paperboard to produce milk containers is one of the largest coating applications. This has almost completely replaced the wax paper carton, because it is a much more durable container. In this as in many other coating applications, the polyethylene coating provides heat seal and barrier properties.

Pouches As a heat seal coating on cellophane, low density polyethylene also provides needed water resistance. This material is used to form pouches for retail packaging of a wide variety of products, foods, candy, etc.

"Skin Pack" Meats Low density polyethylene is coated on polyester or nylon film for the packaging of fresh and processed meats. One example of these nylon containing constructions is the "skin pack" packages of processed meats, where the film is formed against the product for optimum display. Polyester film itself is not thermoplastic enough for any great amount of forming. The polyethylene on the inside seals the package; it also protects the outer ply from the moisture in the meat. These constructions in some cases have a thin vinylidene chloride (PVDC) layer in the center for added resistance to gas permeation.

Industrial Packaging Low density polyethylene is coated onto kraft paper for industrial and heavy duty wrapping. One application is as one or more plys of the multiwall bag, which is very widely used for shipping industrial chemicals, as well as cement, lime, gypsum, fertilizer, and similar products. Some retail packages use this as well.

A recent development in this field is to replace the closely adhered coating with a thin polyolefin film which is tacked to the paper only in spots or lines, leaving the major part free. This gives a better barrier with the same amount of polyolefin, because the paper fibers in the coating tend to penetrate the plastic and permit leakage. The loose film is also more durable because it can stretch when subject to load, while the coating tears with the paper.

Sugar Pouches A very thin low density polyethylene coating is used for the single portion sugar pouches widely found in restaurants. This coating is generally so thin that it is not really waterproof; it is just enough to be heat sealable, and it prevents the sugar from sticking to the paper.

Adhesive Applications Polyethylene is also used as an adhesive between two plys of a laminate. Paper and aluminum foil are joined together, and the resulting construction may also have a polyethylene coating on the outside of the foil layer for heat sealability and mechanical protection. Tobacco pouches, and some food products that require special protection against moisture and gas permeation, such as powdered milk, soup mixes, etc., use this construction.

Boilable Pouches Medium density polyethylene is often applied on polyester film to make "boilable pouches". In this use a prepared or fresh frozen food product is packaged so that it may be placed in boiling water until hot enough to serve. These packages are distributed for retail sales, but the largest customers are restaurants, where the quick preparation of a large variety of dishes without making an accurate estimate of what will be used at any particular meal is needed. The saving in time, storage space, and wastage of left over food far exceeds the cost of the package.

Other Coating Applications Polyethylene coatings are widely used in military packaging, often as a component of complex constructions involving paper, aluminum foil, and fabric.

Photographic supplies are largely packaged in constructions in which polyethylene coating is an essential component, with paper, polyethylene, aluminum foil, polyethylene being a common construction.

White pigmented and other colored polyethylene coatings are used to provide improved appearance as well as barrier properties. Polyethylene coatings on kraft corrugated board are commonly used to improve the moisture resistance of the board and sometimes also the appearance.

Ethylene vinyl acetate copolymers are excellent coating materials and replace polyethylene in many of the above applications where extra toughness, low temperature properties, or abrasion resistance are needed, or where superior adhesion to the substrate is required.

This is a small but rapidly growing segment of the coating field. They also have an advantage where high pigment loadings are required for a very opaque coating, because they can take higher pigment loadings without loss of physical properties.

High density polyethylene gives a coating with improved grease resistance and reduced gas permeability; however, consumption in coatings is still small because of processing difficulties. Most of the high density polyethylene used in coating is blended with low density.

Hot Melt Coatings   Polyolefins, in the form of EVA copolymers, are an important part of a rapidly growing hot melt coating business. Starting out simply as wax additives used to improve wax coatings, EVA containing hot melt coatings have developed into a large family of high grade coatings far superior to wax. These coatings typically consist of a mixture of EVA copolymer, a resin which may be a wood rosin derivative, a hydrocarbon resin, polyterpene resin, or low molecular weight polystyrene and a wax. The wax ordinarily is the major component, but, depending on application, the other components may also be quite large. Similar compositions are also used as hot melt adhesives.

While hot melt coatings are not generally as durable as pure polyolefin extrusion coatings, they can be formulated to serve a wide variety of purposes. They have excellent sealability and show better performance in some high speed sealing operations than polyolefin coatings.

One of their main advantages is that they can be applied by coating equipment, which is less expensive than an extrusion coating line.

Containers and Lids

Reclosable Lids   The largest single item in this category is the low density polyethylene lid used for reclosing coffee cans, shortening cans, and many other kinds of cans. This is a recent and very rapidly growing application, and is in the process of being extended to any canned item, where the contents are not ordinarily used at one time. The can with separate polyethylene lid commonly replaces the key opening type can, which is more expensive, hard to open, and often cuts people. These lids are injection molded on very short cycles, making it possible to produce them in large numbers at a very low cost.

Thermoformed Containers   Low wide containers in quart, pint, and smaller sizes are used for sour cream, cottage cheese, and many prepared foods that require refrigeration but not sterilization. These are made of various plastics, but high density polyethylene is being used in increasing numbers. The margarine tub in particular is being made mainly of high density polyethylene. These containers are generally vacuum formed out of sheeting, although some are injection molded. Injection molding requires thicker walls, so is more expensive but makes a more durable container.

Large scale trial production of lubricating oil cans has been started, using high density polyethylene thermoformed sheet.

Bottles and Tubes

Bleach and Detergent Bottles   High density polyethylene is the large scale blown bottle resin. Bleach and detergent bottles are the largest applications at present. Scouring powder, distilled water, lubricating oil, and many nonfood uses are very common. The light weight and shock resistance give the polyethylene bottle a great advantage over the glass container, especially in larger sizes where the glass bottle is quite fragile.

Drug Bottles   High density polyethylene bottles are also used widely in the packaging of drugs. Recent research has shown that drug preparations that do not have components which permeate polyethylene are protected as well in polyethylene bottles as in glass. This included almost anything in the form of pills or capsules, as well as most dry powders.

The office of the Surgeon General of the Army intiated a study of the compatability and stability of plastic containers for the 96 drugs most widely used by the Army Medical Service.

After a preliminary evaluation of all the possible plastics, it was decided to make the study with high density polyethylene. The reasons for this choice of plastic were economy and utility. At the time the program was initiated, 99% of all plastic bottles were made of polyethylene. While there are other materials that have specific advantages for some special purposes, none of them have a broad enough applicability to warrant large scale investigation.

· Inertness is probably the best single index of the suitability of a material for drug packaging. The fact that the material is inert means that there will be no reaction with the product. If there is a low order of solubility of the product in the polymer, then there will be little permeability or transfer of product through container walls.

The olefins collectively, low and high density polyethylene and polypropylene, are outstanding in chemical resistance. They will dissolve only in hot solvents. If the polyolefins are compared to glass for instance, glass will dissolve in hydrofluoric acid at room temperature, while polyethylene is the standard packaging material for it. Long storage of aqueous solutions in glass containers at room temperature will cause sodium and silicon, as well as other glass components, to dissolve in the solution; nothing of this sort happens with polyethylene.

With the exception of some of the fluorine containing polymers, polyethylene is the most inert available material, and from a practical point of view the cost of the fluorinated polymers is prohibitive.

Water vapor permeability is important in a drug packaging material, and in the study polyethylene was found adequate to the extent that conditioning at 14 and 80 percent relative humidity at the same temperature showed no effect on product stability.

High density polyethylene is a relatively poor barrier to oxygen, yet there was no evidence during the two year study that any of the 96 pharmaceuticals had undergone degradation because of oxygen entry into the package.

While this study does not do away with the necessity of making specific tests with each drug product being considered for packaging, it does show that linear polyethylene has wide application in drug packaging.

Milk Bottles   Linear polyethylene milk bottles have had small scale use for several years. They come in two forms, a returnable bottle for home delivery, which has also had some success in the gallon size in supermarkets, and a light single trip container for the supermarket business. While numerous dairies are using one or the other of these with considerable success, this must still be considered an experimental application. The possibilities inherent in this application will be discussed in the chapter on the future of polyolefins.

The use of polyolefin milk containers is more widespread in Europe, where the single trip container, in the smaller sizes common there, has taken the form of thin walled flexible pouches. This pouch is generally vacuum formed from thin sheet and heat sealed around the edges. It has achieved a considerable degree of sophistication. One form is made from coextruded black and white sheeting, black on the inside to prevent the penetration of light which deteriorates milk flavor, and white on the outside for an attractive appearance. It is often heat sealed and opened by tearing or cutting, because, in Europe where home refrigeration is not common, milk is not usually stored after opening.

Squeeze Bottles   Low density "squeeze bottles" were the first large scale use of polyolefin plastic bottles. In this application the bottle acted as dispenser as well as container, hence justifying the increased cost over glass. Although low density bottles continue to be used at considerable volume, it has been overshadowed by the high density bottle.

Collapsible Tubes   Collapsible tubes made of low density polyethylene are used for shampoos and various paste and cream preparations. This too is a steady but not extremely large volume use.

Closures   This application uses considerable volume of both high and low density polyethylene. The closure may also act as dispenser. Bottle caps and tooth paste tube caps are examples. One advantage of low density polyethylene in these applications is that the material is resilient enough so that it does not require a gasket to form a tight seal. Polyethylene also has a surface that is slippery enough so that the cap does not stick tightly, as caps made of many other materials often do. The light weight and rapid molding cycles possible with low density polyethylene make it one of the most economical closure materials in cost per part.

AUTOMOTIVE APPLICATIONS

The polyolefins have done much to convince the automaker that plastics were not cheap, breakable materials, unsuited to the hard service in an automobile. Automakers show a willingness to examine polyolefin plastics with the idea of using their unique properties to improve quality and cut costs.

An example of this is the polypropylene accelerator pedal with integral hinge. This replaced a molded rubber and metal part, in which the metal hinge very often failed prematurely due to rust and to grit. The hinge in the polypropylene pedal is a thin area in the plastic, which has excellent flex life and is completely immune to corrosion or dirt. Another recent application based on the same property is an injection molded glove box with integral molded hinge.

Other polypropylene applications are an injection molded arm rest insert, and an injection molded heater deflector. A glass filled polypropylene formulation has been successful as a fan shroud. Expanded, rubber modified polypropylene has been used for a sun visor.

Linear polyethylene has been used for cowl side kick panels. The traditional painted hardboard rapidly deteriorated in service. The injection molded polyolefin plastic part was molded in color to match the interior and required no painting. Incorporating the windlace at one edge eliminated the need of a separate windlace, so a great improvement in quality was accomplished at no net cost increase.

Thermoformed linear polyethylene truck door trim panels have also been successful. Die-cut polyethylene foam has seen considerable use in body gasketry, like that used to seal tail lamps.

The largest single polyolefin piece used in an automobile is the linear polyethylene fender filler plate, which weighss up to six pounds. This is the plate that fits between the fender and the wheel, forming the wheel well. The polyolefin plate is completely corrosion resistant, which is very important in this location, for it is constantly exposed to moisture and corrosive materials, such as the salts used for de-icing roads. The plastic requires no protective finish and does not show the tendency to rattle that metal plates have. It has so far only been used on a few cars, but it appears to be very satisfactory.

Polypropylene has been used in a variety of spots, such as an air conditioner blower wheel, air conditioner and defroster ducts, and for the backs of bucket seats.

HOUSEWARES

A wide variety of containers ranging from garbage cans through wash baskets, wastebaskets, hampers, on down to freezer containers, bowls, pitchers, and finally to salt or spice shakers are all made of polyethylene. Generally, a mixture of high and low density is used for injection molding these items. Some are made by blow molding, and the material is then pure linear polyethylene.

Polypropylene has recently moved into this area on a large scale, both in the traditional lines and in some specialty items using its particular properties. For instance, a line of syrup servers uses the molded hinge to cover the pouring spout. The exceptional ability of polypropylene to reproduce mold surface finishes is used in wood grain and other special surface finishes which give the parts a high style appearance. The wood grain finish has appeared on a wide variety of items not merely in the kitchen but appropriate to other rooms as well.

1967 polyolefin consumption in millions of pounds is given in Table 6.2.

TABLE 6.2.   Polyolefins Used in Housewares (in million pounds)

Polyethylene, high density	100
Polyethylene, low density	210
Polypropylene	47

APPLIANCES

Polyolefins are still a relatively small factor in the appliance field, but they are growing more rapidly than the major competitors in this field.

Major Appliances

Table 6.3 shows polyolefin consumption in major appliances in 1967 in millions of pounds.

TABLE 6.3.   Polyolefins Used in Major Appliances (in million pounds)

Polypropylene	27.1
High density polyethylene	1.0

This polyethylene figure includes only molded parts and does not include film used for waterproofing insulation, wrapping, etc.

Polypropylene is a favorite material for washing machine agitators, for baskets in dishwashers, driers and clothes washers, and in general for any application requiring resistance to water, heat, and detergents. It is also used for pumps, fans, fan shrouds, and for many small parts.

In one dishwasher there are 23 parts made of glass reinforced polypropylene.

Small Appliances

The small appliances, vacuum cleaners, blenders, and mixers, can openers, electric knives, vibrators, electric tooth brushes, razors, etc., also consume a good deal of polyolefin plastic. Table 6.4 shows 1967 figures.

TABLE 6.4.   Polyolefins Used in Small Appliances 1967 (in million pounds)

Polypropylene	10.2
Polyethylene	2.0

The polyolefins are used for housings, cabinets, handles, knobs, and decorative features.

BUILDING CONSTRUCTION

The polyolefins do not have a very large share of the huge construction market. Their largest single use in this field is as film for vapor barrier. 1967 consumption is given in Table 6.5.

TABLE 6.5.   Polyolefins Used in Building Construction (in million pounds)

Polyethylene vapor barrier	58
Polyethylene pipe, fittings, conduits	4
Polyethylene profile extrusion	4

The vapor barrier is of low density polyethylene film, the profile extrusions are of linear, and the pipe, fittings and conduits are of both. The use of copolymers of ethylene and polar monomers in some of the flexible profile extrusions used for gasketing and sealing is growing. It replaces flexible vinyl in these applications and achieves better low temperature flexibility and longer service life.

Chlorinated polyethylene is starting to be used in the roofing of commercial buildings, but this is not yet a large use.

The growing use of cross-linked polyethylene in insulating electrical wire will be discussed under electrical applications.

TOYS

The polyolefins are a considerable part of the plastics used in toys. In 1967 the following consumptions were recorded, as shown in Table 6.6.

TABLE 6.6.   Polyolefins Used in Toys (in million pounds)

Low density polyethylene	90
High density polyethylene	41
Polypropylene	40

The polyolefins are the fastest growing material in this toy field, reflecting a continuing trend towards upgrading toys and making them safer.

The most popular method of fabrication is injection molding, and a tremendous number of injection molded polyolefin toys is on the market. Blow molding is also used. Doll bodies are made in this way generally from linear polyethylene. Blocks, toy vehicle bodies, boats, and similar items are also blow molded.

EVA copolymers are finding a small market in specialty items that require extra flexibility, like bellows, and for movable parts.

ARTIFICIAL FLOWERS

Injection molded low density polyethylene artificial flowers and plants have nearly replaced all other kinds of artificial flowers. They are available in realistic copies of natural flowers, and also in imaginative forms unlike anything that has ever grown. Plants of considerable size are used to decorate hotel and store lobbies almost to the exclusion of real plants.

Since these flowers and plants are usually made by the assembly of individual petals and leaves, a great deal of hand labor is involved. For this reason they are usually made in places where labor is cheap. Hong Kong has been the center of the polyethylene flower market for many years.

ELECTRICAL USES

Wire and cable is a large consumer of polyolefins. In 1967 the volume of polyethylene used was approximately as shown in Table 6.7.

TABLE 6.7.   Polyethylene Used in Wire and Cable (in million pounds)

Low density	185
High density	50
Foamed	10
Cross-linked	35

The main use for the low density polyethylene was in telephone cable insulation and jacketing. High density polyethylene was used for jacketing of buried cables, particularly those conforming to specifications of the Rural Electrification Administration (REA), because of its improved abrasion resistance. Foamed polyethylene was used mainly for the dielectric in coaxial cable, and its big use was for cable TV installations.

Cross-linkable polyethylene has become the main material used for the outer jacketing of power cable. This use is growing very rapidly because of the underground residential distribution (URD) program, the program for burying power distribution lines in residential areas, both for new construction and for area renovation. Cross-linkable polyethylene is also rapidly displacing rubber and vinyl in the medium voltage power distribution field.

Ethylene vinyl acetate (EVA) copolymers with a low level of comonomer are replacing low density polyethylene in some of its largest scale uses, like in telephone cable sheathing, because of their superior low temperature flexibility and resistance to stress cracking.

Polyolefins are also finding their way into new electrical applications, such as being substrates for flexible circuits, where polyethylene, polypropylene, and ethylene ethyl acrylic (EEA) copolymers have been used. These flexible circuits are being considered for the replacement of conventional automotive wiring, as well as for the electronics industry where they are now being used.

During the past year a new method for soldering multilayer circuit boards was developed. This consists of a sheet of radiation cross-linked polyolefin which has precisely formed pockets containing balls of solder. When heated, the polyolefin shrinks and forces the solder up into minute termination points. This is said to give superior soldering due to the ability of the polyolefin to "pump" the solder into place when hot.

Agricultural Applications

Polyolefins, especially low density polyethylene, have a considerable use for agricultural purposes. The largest of these is for agricultural mulches, in which a sheet of plastic is laid down the row in a field, and the crop is planted through holes in the plastic. Special machinery has been devised to lay the plastic down very rapidly, and at the same time to turn a strip of dirt over both edges to hold it down. This mulch increases soil temperature early in the season, conserves water, prevents soil caking and packing, and reduces fertilizer washout. In many crops the increased yields outweigh the considerable cost of the mulch. Strawberries, for instance, are commercially grown on polyethylene in most cases. In this crop the advantage of keeping the berries clean, and making them easier to pick is also important.

The polyethylene film greenhouse is quite widely used. It is inexpensive and produces interior conditions very well suited to a wide variety of crops. Tomatoes, for instance, are grown in considerable quantity under polyethylene.

These houses are generally of light frame construction and in cold areas will consist of a layer of polyethylene film both outside the frame and inside, leaving an air space for insulation. The greenhouse may be heated by warm air distributed through polyethylene tubing ducts. In regions of heavy sunlight exposure a polyethylene film cover usually lasts only a season, but in northern countries where the summers are cool and short they may last several years. It is also possible to put an ultraviolet light inhibitor in the film to increase its life.

Polyolefin film also has many uses on the farm for the temporary protection of materials and produce.

It is possible, for instance, to make a "silo" that satisfactorily stores ensilage, simply by putting down a sheet of heavy gage polyethylene film, piling the ensilage on the sheet, and covering this with another sheet, sealing the edges by folding them together and covering them with dirt. Black film is necessary at least for the top sheet because light will spoil the ensilage. A "silo" of this sort will keep fodder in good condition for an entire winter. It is inexpensive to make, and it may be placed near either where the crop was grown, or where it will be used, to reduce the hauling.

Wire mesh coops for chickens and other small animals can be wrapped with polyethylene film in severe weather for protection.

The nursery industry uses polyolefin film and polyolefin coated paper to a great extent. The roots of dug plants and in many cases the entire plant are protected from drying by a polyethylene bag or a wrapping of polyethylene coated paper.

Polyethylene film is also used as a waterproofing liner for farm ponds and irrigation ditches to prevent water loss.

Bags made of oriented polyolefin tapes are finding increased use as heavy duty sacking, and for use as sand bags for flood protection, and even for permanent water control purposes.

Polyethylene pipe is widely used for irrigation and for farm water systems. Its flexibility makes it very convenient for use in wells because continuous lengths for the entire depth of the well can be used. For use with the popular jet well system, a special form of pipe containing both a small high pressure tube and a larger low pressure tube, all made in one piece, makes installation possible in smaller bores than possible with two separate pipes.

Pipe made of very high molecular weight linear polyethylene is finding increased application. Lacking the flexibility of low density pipe, it must be used in straight lengths like metal pipe, and hence, requires many couplings in a long run. It is much stronger; it can be used for higher pressures; and it can withstand domestic hot water temperatures. While not yet a large factor in the plastics pipe business, it is growing rapidly.

Very large high density polyethylene pipe, with diameters up to 40 inches, is made for irrigation purposes. While pipe of this size is not flexible in the usual sense, it is flexible enough so that long sections extending over many freight cars can be moved by rail. The pipe can flex enough to permit the train to round any curve.

SUMMARY

This has been a very brief discussion of some major polyolefin uses. It does not claim to be comprehensive but it does indicate the extent to which the polyolefin plastics have penetrated almost every aspect of modern life.

Some predictions of their spread in the future are given in the next chapter.

SEVEN

the future of polyolefin plastics

ECONOMIC DEVELOPMENTS

The polyolefins are currently at the beginning of the most far reaching changes that have ever been witnessed in an industry. The exact timing and details of these changes cannot be predicted, but their magnitude and their impact on the general economy are already becoming apparent.

One of the most significant factors influencing the future growth of polyolefin plastics is cost. Up to this time plastics have been relatively expensive materials that have obtained their markets because of their special properties or their efficient processing. Continuing cost reductions in the polyolefin plastics, running counter to continuing cost increases in practically every other major material of construction, are changing these price relationships.

Monomer Cost Trends

Looking into the future, it appears very likely that plastics production costs will continue to decline, and this is particularly true for polyolefins. There has been a tremendous increase in ethylene production capacity in recent years. This capacity has been in the form of very large single train production lines, with much lower production costs than lines built earlier. Since markets for the new capacity are not yet visible, it appears likely that there will be a great over-capacity of ethylene. This situation will almost inevitably bring ethylene prices down nearly to the low production costs of the new plants. Since many of the new ethylene plants may at the same time also produce propylene, a similar situation is developing with this monomer. The production methods for other olefin monomers are undergoing parallel cost reductions. Most of the other monomers for thermoplastics start out with an ethylene base. They will also benefit from the cost reduction of this material, but percentage wise this will make less difference, because the subsequent chemical processes do not have the same sort of volume and so cannot attain the same production economies. This means that the already low monomer cost base of the polyolefins will not only fall lower, but will also be lower in comparison with that of its major competitors in the plastics field.

Polymerization Costs

At the same time new polymerization techniques are reducing the polymerization costs of polyolefins. The tremendous strides achieved in the understanding of catalysts, for instance, makes it possible to produce catalysts so efficient that the costly catalyst removal steps, heretofore needed for linear polyethylene and polypropylene, can be eliminated, and this ability will undoubtedly soon be extended to all polyolefins. Revolutionary processes also being developed will eliminate the use of solvent in the low pressure polymerization processes. Solvent removal, losses, and reclamation now constitute some of the greatest costs of these processes. The "dry" polymerization processes will completely eliminate these costs. Some of these processes are already commercial on a small scale in Europe and give indication of costs far below the conventional ones. At present the range of polymer produced is limited, but there appears to be a good chance that full product lines can eventually be made by them. This will bring polyolefin prices to a level competitive with many very inexpensive traditional materials in large volume applications.

Most of the traditional construction materials, on the other hand, have already been through the major cost reduction revolutions. They are now coming up against depletion of the least expensive sources, and have no more means of combatting production cost increases due to general inflationary pressures. Similarly, the means of using traditional materials have been thoroughly explored and cannot be expected to show far-reaching innovations in the future. Polyolefin plastics, on the other hand, are still very new materials whose applicability and processing are just beginning to be explored.

The Price-Volume Relationship

A recent article pointed out the close correlation between price and volume in a plastic. If the price in cents per pound of a plastic material is plotted on a logarithmic plot against volume in pounds per year, it is found that plastics all very nearly fall on a straight line, volume increasing as price decreases. The interesting fact is that materials like the light metals, and even steel and iron, generally follow the same line. It appears very probable that as plastics decrease in price, they will increase in volume, while the traditional construction materials will follow the same line in the opposite direction.

One of the misleading factors in a price per pound comparison of polyolefin plastics with metals is the difference in specific gravity. For a great many things that could be made, either of metal or plastic, it is the volume of the part that is significant and not its weight, so that the price per unit volume is the competitive factor. Polyolefins are the lightest of all the plastics, so their price per unit volume is in fact lower than the per pound price would indicate, and their production in terms of volume is proportionally even greater than their production in pounds.

At present, world plastics production slightly exceeds the production of all nonferrous metals in pounds but is three times as great in terms of volume. It is estimated that early in the 1980's plastics volume will be greater than all metals including the ferrous, although, of course, the poundage will be smaller. It appears inevitable that a large part of this huge volume will be polyolefin plastics.

The polyolefin rubbers and the polyolefin fibers have already started to remake their entire industries on the basis of a whole new relationship between cost and value, which is rapidly pushing traditional materials from large markets.

The polyolefin plastics have achieved their great expansion without a similarly spectacular upset of established values, because their impact has been spread over a broad group of industries whose total volume greatly exceeds that of the polyolefin plastics, and whose materials base consists of low cost materials.

These are low cost, high volume industries, many of them highly tradition bound and firmly committed to specific materials. For example, construction, packaging, automotive, and furniture all have experienced more or less penetration by polyolefins, but all of them are still largely served by traditional materials.

The coming great growth in polyolefin plastics will be the replacement in major markets of wood, paper, and metals.

DEVELOPMENT IN RESINS

It is almost impossible to separate resin developments from the processing methods now under development. To a great extent it is new resin developments that make possible revolutionary processing changes. The ability of the polyolefin producer to tailor a resin to meet specific use requirements has progressed enormously. Copolymerization and methods of controlling the details of molecular configuration are well advanced. Gel chromatography, a rapid new method for determining molecular weight distribution, has made accurate control of this important property possible. Advances in the understanding of polymer degradation mechanisms has made it possible to improve the service life of polyolefin parts to the point where they may soon become some of the most permanent materials of construction available.

Some of the details of how resin developments affect processing methods will be mentioned as the new processing methods are discussed.

DEVELOPMENTS IN PROCESSING METHODS

Some of the developments that will make up the processing technology of the future are as follows: the vulcanization or cross-linking of polyolefins to improve their heat resistance and to protect them from the adverse effects of certain environments; the development of polyolefin foams, both structural and low density, to improve the strength and volume to weight ratios and to add thermal insulation value; the development of composite materials wherein the easy fabrication and processing characteristics of the polyolefins are combined with the high strength of materials not readily processed. Ultra high molecular weight polyolefins with greater strength and resistance to deterioration are also being developed.

Cross-Linking

Cross-linking of polyolefins by the use of peroxide cross-linking agents is already a commercial process of considerable size, but it has certain disadvantages, like relatively slow speed, the high cost of the active agents, and the fact that the agents leave undesirable residues in the polymer. Two entirely different cross-linking methods are under active development and may soon change the position of cross-linked polyolefins entirely.

The most exciting of these, and in many ways the most promising, is radition cross-linking. Until recently high energy radiation was so expensive that its industrial use was practical only for very special purposes. This field has developed so rapidly that it is now possible to purchase reliable and relatively inexpensive radiation sources capable of irradiation cross-linking polyolefins at costs entirely competitive with chemical means. It is almost certain that in a very short time the cost will be down to the point where it can greatly increase the market potential of cross-linked polyolefins. Radiation cross-linking is very rapid and leaves no objectionable residues which might impart color or odor to the product.

The other important cross-linking method comes from the rapid development of copolymerization techniques. The polyolefin rubbers have shown that diolefins may be polymerized with olefins to give sulfur vulcanizable rubbers. The same may be done with polyolefin plastics. In this way, of course, the dividing line between rubbers and plastics will be even more blurred and the question of whether a particular material is a soft plastic or a hard rubber will become purely academic. However, the economic impact of rapid and inexpensive cross-linkable polyolefins will be tremendous.

Structural Foams

Polyolefin structural foams differ greatly from familiar foamed plastics and show promise of much broader applications. While several developments are under way, the most promising one appears to be a modification of conventional injection molding, in which a molten mass of resin containing gas or volatile liquid is injected into a mold cavity. Up to the time of injection, the mass is kept under high enough pressure to prevent expansion of the gas. When the material enters the mold, the pressure is released and the gas expands. The amount injected is only enough to fill the cavity after the expansion of the gas has taken place. This method produces a relatively dense foam, but the important point is that it has a skin of essentially un-expanded resin. The mold cavity is cooled, so the material in contact with the cavity does not expand as much as the relatively hot interior. This produces a part where most of the strength is on the surface where it is most needed, while the interior is a relatively light struc-ture which serves only to stiffen the surface. This makes very efficient use of the strength of the material, yet the part is light enough to be quite inexpensive.

Reinforced Polyolefins

The development of composite materials with polyolefin resins as the plastic part is still very new but has enormous potential. Glass fiber reinforced polyolefins are not new, but the developments that promise to make them mass production materials are new. One of these is the development of coatings for the glass fiber that give a true reinforcing effect. Up to this time the bond between polyolefins and glass has been quite weak, and full composite strength proper-ties could not be developed, but now strong bonds and full reinforce-ment are possible. Another development is the direct injection mold-ing of dry blends of polyolefin powders and glass fibers. Previously the glass fibers were hot compounded into the resin. This degraded the strength of the fiber and added to the cost of the mixture. It has been found that this is not merely unnecessary but harmful, and dry blends mold more readily than precompounded granules. One of the surprising things about these compounds is that even blends con-taining rather large percentages of glass will mold almost as easily as unfilled resin. Extruding such a mixture at low shear rates in a compounding extruder requires a great deal more pressure than extruding the resin, but at the extremely high shear rates found in an injection machine, the material flows very freely. The glass fibers seem to float along in the melt under these conditions without greatly influencing the flow properties and without greatly degrading the fibers. The combined effect of the lower cost and better performance of these filled polyolefins should open up large new uses.

Processing High Molecular Weight Resins

Many of the methods for producing polyolefin plastics can quite conveniently produce resins of extremely high molecular weight. In spite of their superior properties these materials have not found any considerable applications, because of the difficulty of processing them by the conventional methods. The growth anticipated in these materials is not, in fact, due to new qualities in the resins, but rather to new processing methods that are practicable and will decrease the cost of processing conventional resins.

Solid State Methods   These new processing methods avoid the relatively slow melting and cooling stages which have been traditional in polyolefin plastic processing, and substitute rapid solid state operations which greatly increase production speed. These methods are adaptations of highly successful methods used for traditional materials.

Cold Stamping   An example is cold stamping. High density polyethylene-polypropylene copolymer formulations that can be formed into shape by cold stamping are already available. Their further development will open wide markets.

A corporation has been formed to produce a glass fiber reinforced thermoplastic sheet using polypropylene as the resin. This sheet is trademarked Azdel * and is formed by metal stamping equipment as fast as metal parts are stamped. It can be formed in a single set of water cooled matched metal dies on an 8-10 second cycle, whereas steel is formed in a series of from 4-6 dies taking almost as long on each one. Savings on die costs in auto production runs of under 100,000 model units would offset the higher cost of the thermoplastic sheet.

The high heat distortion temperature of the Azdel * sheet should allow it to resist automobile paint oven heats of from 235°-350°F.

---

* Trademark of G.R.T.L. Company.

When polypropylene is used as base resin, it has a heat distortion temperature of 327°F.

Drop Forging   Another example is drop forging, in which a warm billet is shaped almost instantaneously into a complex shape by a cold die suddenly impacted upon it. This process not only allows very rapid production but modifies the structure of the material to produce greatly improved strength.

Folding Boxes   The traditional cut and crease operation of the paperboard industry is readily adaptable to polyolefin sheeting and is capable of producing rigid packages of many shapes at extremely high rates of speed. A few successful applications have already been made.

Direct Fluff Processing   In addition, the traditional processing methods are being developed in ways that reduce cost and improve properties. For instance, the powder blend technique widely used in PVC is being adapted to polyolefins. In this technique the traditional fluxing operation which produces a polyolefin pellet is by-passed, and the raw powder from the reactor is dry blended with the necessary additives and used directly in the processing operation. This not only reduces resin cost by eliminating a processing operation, but also makes a product of improved properties by reducing the length of time that the resin is exposed to processing temperatures.

These are, of course, all in addition to the normal advances both in resin developments and in traditional processing machinery, which are constantly lowering cost and improving quality.

OPPOSING DEVELOPMENTS

In opposition to these trends are the rapid advances made by other plastic materials. The great packaging film and blown bottle applications, which have for several years been largely in polyolefins, are coming under serious attack by other resins, especially PVC. Developments in PVC have to some extent paralleled those in polyolefins. The shift from acetylene to ethylene as a base hydrocarbon for the monomer, and the development of processes that do not require use or disposal of large amounts of HCl have greatly reduced monomer costs. Similarly, the development of bulk polymerization should considerably reduce the cost of this step as well. However, similar strides have not been made against the high cost of stabilization and against high processing costs. PVC will undoubtedly grow rapidly, but not in a way to limit the polyolefins seriously.

FUTURE MARKETS

This very general discussion of possible trends should be balanced by a brief look at the short term picture. The growth trends in already well established markets may be extrapolated for a short distance to give a good estimate of the situation in the next few years.

Packaging

Simple extrapolation of growth in the packaging area shows us that there will be a great increase in the field, the largest in film, with blown containers nearly as great, and lesser amounts of increase in injection molded containers and closures. Some recent estimates are shown in Table 7.1.

TABLE 7.I.   Growth of Polyolefins in Packaging (in million pounds)

	1967	1970 est.
Polyethylene film	800	1500
Polypropylene film	61	100
Polyethylene coatings	307	360
EVA copolymer	20	45
Polyolefin molded and formed containers	100	175
Polyethylene bottles, high and low density	350	710
Polyolefin closures	44	67

Bottles   A little longer look shows that the blown bottle has greater possibilities in many largely untouched fields; milk bottles are a familiar possibility that would be larger than any current plastic bottle application. Much development work has been done, and the question seems to be merely that of finding the best approach.

Polyethylene milk bottles are being used in two forms, a light weight single trip container for the supermarket trade, and a heavier multiple trip container for home delivery. At present the multiple trip container shows the best economics. The plastic container cannot stand the stream sterilization used on glass bottles, so new methods of sterilization have been developed and are very satisfactory. The fairly heavy multiple trip polyethylene milk bottle is competitive in cost with a glass bottle and will average many more trips than the glass bottle. It also simplifies handling, especially of empties, and is less noisy.

The single trip container has to compete with the inexpensive polyethylene coated paperboard carton. At its present state of development the board carton is a very satisfactory container in all sizes below a gallon. In the gallon size there is some problem with leakage and with breakage on handling. This means that if the gallon all polyethylene bottle can be brought to a price nearly competitive with the carton, it could become accepted on a service basis. Most of the current activity represents attempts to overcome the cost problem.

In this intensely competitive situation, shipping costs are an important factor. The possibility of making polyolefin milk bottles at the place of use, using automated yet relatively inexpensive equipment, is a real advantage, considering that glass bottles are inevitably tied to a large production facility. One of the major obstacles to this approach is the required investment. Few dairies are in a position to make the necessary investment in production facilities. Some resin producers are trying to solve this problem. One experimental method is having the bottle producing machinery at the dairy, but owned and operated by the resin producer who sells the dairy the bottles made. For the dairy this is similar to buying bottles from an outside source, except that there is no shipping cost. Other people are experimenting with leasing arrangements. It is quite likely that a practical solution to this problem will soon be found, and large volumes of polyolefins will go into milk bottles.

The broader field of beverage bottling is much more distant, but not improbable. Improved strength resin makes economical wall thickness possible for carbonated beverages, and relatively inexpensive interior coatings can make CO_2 retention acceptable for short storage items. A beer bottle is farther afield because beer is pasturized, so that at the very least an inexpensive cross-linking method would be required to give the necessary heat resistance, unless, of course, a resin like poly-4-methylpentene could be made at a low enough price. Also, some beer is now stabilized by very fine filtration instead of pasteurization. This trend could favor a plastic bottle.

Folding Cartons   The plastic sheet carton could hardly expect to compete with paperboard in applications like soap, where paperboard alone is an adequate container. But in many cases, like cake mix, where an inner sealed container is needed inside the paperboard with an additional paper wrap outside that, it is entirely possible that a polyolefin sheet carton could be substituted economically.

Film   Polyolefin film will replace paper in many packaging applications. Large volume mailers have already started using polyethylene film in the wrapping of packages for mailing. The sack for groceries at the supermarket is another likely replacement area.

Supermarket Grocery Sack   A low density polyethylene sack is cheaper and more durable than the Kraft paper now used, mainly because it is not weakened by moisture from refrigerated or frozen foods, and is more resistant to puncture by sharp objects. The problem is that it is too limp to fill readily. Intensive work is being done on equipment that will enable a packer to fill a polyethylene bag as fast or even faster than the paper sack can now be filled.

When the practicality of this equipment has been satisfactorily demonstrated, there will probably be a rapid expansion of this use for polyethylene film.

A smaller related use, the sack used by the customer for containing self-service fruits and produce, is rapidly being taken over by polyethylene bags. In this case the main incentive is that the transparent bag prevents pilferage by hiding merchandise under the produce.

Can Bundling   The use of a heavy gage shrink film overwrap on cans to replace the traditional corrugated board carton has been successful on a test basis. In this packaging method a shallow corrugated board tray is used to align the layer of cans. A tube of heavy polyolefin shrink film is placed around the cans and base, and the assembly is run through an oven to shrink the film. The shrinkage of the film holds cans and tray tightly together to form a solid, easily handled packaged. These cases can be stacked as readily as the traditional cases and protect the cans as well as cartons do. A short vertical slit in the plastic opens the case more rapidly than a carton can be opened, and the shallow base tray can be placed directly on the store shelves without the individual handling of cans that is now necessary. There have also been successful applications where the board tray was eliminated.

Pallet Wrapping   A similar technique for fastening pallet loads is also under development. The articles to be palletized are stacked on the pallet, a tube of shink film is placed around the whole assembly, and the film is then shrunk in an oven or by a hot air blast, holding pallet and load tightly together. This replaces metal strapping with much less damage to the packages, and also gives considerable protection against mechanical damage and soiling. Once the shrinking ovens have been installed, savings are realized from reduced labor and less damage. Both of these are very large scale uses that could be realized in the near future.

Automotive

The steady penetration of polyolefins into the automotive market is being accelerated by the development of plating techniques, which will permit the use of polyolefin plastics on all exterior trim, as well as interior trim and finish items.

Even major body panels are no longer as improbable as they seemed only very recently. Structural foams and glass filled polyolefins present a real possibility of matching the cost performance relation of steel before long, particularly as high speed processing methods develop.

A recent application of linear polyethylene as automotive fender filler plates is the largest single item, in terms of pounds per car, that has yet been developed. This could well be the start of the use of polyolefins on a large scale in automotive structures.

There has been a great deal of interest in fuel tanks made of polyolefin plastics. The German Porsche sports cars use a fuel tank of linear polyethylene. One advantage is that they can readily be made in complex shapes to fit available spaces. This becomes increasingly important with the sophistication of automotive design, hence the fuel tank could well grow to be a large application. Gasoline loss by permeation is solved by means of special coatings.

Furniture

Growth in the areas of mass seating in stadiums and assembly halls can readily be predicted, but the real change has only begun. This is the replacement of the traditional hardwood frame of upholstered furniture with structural foam. Structural foam made from other plastics is commercial; polyolefin structural foam is well developed but not yet commercial in any quantity. The ability to put finishes on this material that closely resemble traditional wood finishes makes it very easy to produce an entire plastic frame at lower cost and with better properties than the wood. The highly traditional furniture business does not yield readily to change, but it appears very likely that eventually most furniture will be polyolefin or other plastic in basic construction, with traditional materials used only as decoration.

Building Construction

The role of polyolefins in construction has so far been limited mainly to film, which is used as waterproofing membrane in various locations, but a much greater role is opening up.

Interior Trim   The ability to simulate the most expensive wood finishes in structural polyolefin foam leads to the possibility of using this on a large scale for interior trim, wall and ceiling paneling, doors, door and window frames. The greatest advantage would come from preformed and preassembled units, which would be inexpensively made by mass production techniques. Structural foam assemblies have the advantage over wooden preassemblies in being lighter in weight and less prone to damage during transportation. Structural foam has the added advantage of being fairly compatible with ordinary carpenter work. That is to say, it can be sawed with a standard wood saw and can be nailed or screwed into place with standard wood screws. This endows the preformed piece with some flexibility, since it can be modified and fitted on the spot to some extent, and it can easily be fastened to ordinary frame construction with tools readily available.

Piping   Polyolefin piping has not been suitable for standard interior plumbing because its heat resistance is inadequate for hot water service. This situation is rapidly being remedied with the development of cross-linked polyethylene pipe, which has excellent heat resistance. It is possible that some of the ultra-high molecular weight linear resins will be adequate for this purpose. As soon as the practicality of the polyolefin pipe for hot water is clearly established, the rapidly increasing cost of copper should open an enormous market.

Plumbing Fixtures   The closely allied field of plumbing fixtures has already been penetrated by high cost engineering plastics, which are competitive because of the increasing cost of brass, the traditional material. To the extent that these plastics are inherently high in cost, and not merely temporarily high priced because of lack of competition and undeveloped production methods, they must be considered merely as interim materials. The high costs of developing a new technology, which initially will offer only small volume markets, is more readily borne by a high priced specialty plastic than by a low cost high volume material. However, after the initial transition from metal to plastic is well advanced, the advantage of the high cost material is no longer great enough to offset the cost, and inexpensive materials like the polyolefins will be found to be quite adequate. This will almost certainly be true in plumbing fixtures, where the currently preferred plastics really have very little property advantage over many polyolefins, and are decidedly inferior in moisture resistance.

As in the automotive field the growing ability to put durable metal plating on polyolefins will help open these markets.

Building Wiring   The rapid growth of cross-linked polyethylene wire insulation will very soon enter this into strong competition with the vinyl insulated wire, at present the main wire used in buildings. There is little question that once this industry is well developed, the cross-linked polyolefin will have both price and property advantages over vinyl.

Siding   The building siding market is at present penetrated only by PVC and fluorinated polymers because of their superior weathering resistance, and this is likely to continue to be the case in the near future. However, the inherent weatherability of polyolefins is not inferior to that of PVC. Thus, in the not too distant future, when developments in the protection of polyolefins against the effects of weather have progressed further, there is a good possibility of developments in this field as well.

In conclusion it appears that, except for the basic load bearing structures, which will undoubtedly continue to be wood, steel, or concrete for a long time to come, polyolefins have a good chance of wide applications in building construction.

Appliance Markets

Almost without most people becoming aware of it, the household appliance business has shifted from a metal and wood based industry to a plastics based industry. The plastics used are not predominantly polyolefins at this stage of development. The large area, appearance oriented applications, housings cases, covers, grilles, etc., are mainly in impact polystyrene and copolymers of styrene. However, linear polyethylene, polypropylene, and copolymers of ethylene and propylene, are starting to penetrate these markets, and have definite advantages in heat resistance, impact strength, and other properties. It is probable that this penetration will increase in the future.

Similarly, motor housings, piping, valves, gears, and other high performance applications are now mainly in "engineering plastics" like nylon, polycarbonate and the like. The development of high performance polyolefins has advanced and will certainly accelerate; and then many of these applications will by force of economics gradually be taken over by polyolefins. It has been estimated that by 1970 polypropylene will be the third most widely used plastic in the appliance industry, still considerably below polystyrene, but probably quite close to the second, which will be acrylonitrile-butadiene-styrene resins (ABS).

SUMMARY

It may appear that this chapter has described an impossibly favorable growth situation for the polyolefin plastics. However, it has been the history of these materials to outrun the most optimistic predictions. There is little doubt that the materials revolution, which is replacing all the familiar construction materials with synthetic materials, is well on its way. The coming age will be the plastics age, and polyolefin plastics will play a very large part in it.

Index